Banking Reforms and Monetary Policy
in the People's Republic of China

Banking Reforms and Monetary Policy in the People's Republic of China

Is the Chinese Central Banking System Ready for Joining the WTO?

Yong Guo

First published 2002 by
PALGRAVE MACMILLAN
Houndmills, Basingstoke, Hampshire RG21 6XS and
175 Fifth Avenue, New York, N.Y. 10010
Companies and representatives throughout the world

PALGRAVE MACMILLAN is the global academic imprint of the Palgrave Macmillan division of St. Martin's Press LLC and of Palgrave Macmillan Ltd. Macmillan® is a registered trademark in the United States, United Kingdom and other countries. Palgrave is the registered trademark in the European Union and other countries.

ISBN 1–4039–0078–7

This book is printed on paper suitable for recycling and made from fully managed and sustained forest sources.

A catalogue record for this book is available from the British Library.

Library of Congress Cataloging-in-Publication Data

Guo, Yong, 1968-
    Banking reforms and monetary policy in PR China: is the Chinese central banking system ready for joining the WTO? / Yong Guo.
      p. cm.
    Includes bibliographical references and index.
    ISBN 1–4039–0078–7

      1. Banks and banking, Central—China. 2. Banks and banking—China. 3. Monetary policy—China. 4. Finance—China. 5. Commercial credit—China. 6. Agricultural credit—China. 7. China—Economic policy—1976–2000. 8. China—Economic policy—2000-9. World Trade Orgainzation. I. Title.

HG3336 .G86 2002
332.1'1'0951—dc21

2002072117

10 9 8 7 6 5 4 3 2 1
11 10 09 08 07 06 05 04 03 02

Printed and bound in Great Britain by
Antony Rowe Ltd, Chippenham, Wiltshire

To the central bankers and reformers in the People's Republic of China

Contents

List of Figures

List of Tables

List of Boxes

Preface

This study of Chinese banking reforms and monetary policy analyses the decentralization of the Chinese financial system between 1978 and 2001. It examines the Chinese central bank's monetary policy tools such as the central bank's exclusive control over the setting of interest rates, reserve ratio requirements, the creation of an inter-bank money market, and the implementation of open market operations. The work discusses the economic models proposed in the academic literature which include financial decentralization such as stop–go cycles and gradual reform theory in the formerly centrally planned system. Challenges that Chinese banks will face after the People's Republic of China (PRC) joins the World Trade Organization are discussed. These challenges include financial risks, the default loan issue, and the bankruptcy issue.

The study begins with a discussion of the centrally planned economy and its structure in the PRC (the monobank). It has shown that the PRC used the credit plan and cash plan to control the economy before 1978. After economic reform, the commercial banking and policy banking functions were separated from the central bank. The separation facilitated sound financial intermediation, reinforcement of bank supervision, and regulatory direction. The People's Bank of China (PBC) became an independent central bank, relatively free from the government's political influence. The PBC uses different monetary policy tools to control economic growth. In 1993 the PBC used interest rates to control inflation. In 1994 the foreign exchange rate restriction was eased. The monetary policy target was changed to maintenance of exchange rate stability. In response to this change, the PBC tested money supply as a tool to conduct open market operations in 1995. Because of the immaturity of the inter-bank lending market and the small size of the treasury bill market, open market operation ceased.

In 1998 the state eliminated loan ceilings for commercial banks and their removal stimulated commercial banking reform. As the gradual development of the inter-bank lending market and the treasury bill market proceeded, the central bank re-established open market operations. The progress in reform successfully isolated the PRC from the Asian Financial Crisis in 1997. The Chinese economy remained fairly stable during the Asian Financial Crisis between July 1997 and July

1998. The reform between 1998 and 2001 emphasized bank supervision, resolving the 'bad' loan issue, and the control of deflation.

This study concludes that the reforms implemented between 1978 and 2000 had a significant positive impact on the Chinese banking system. The Chinese central bank chose the right monetary policy tools. The study also supports the McKinnon (1993) theory of financial liberalization: There is an 'optimum order' in the financial reform of formerly centrally planned economies. This work concludes that between 1949 and 2001 Chinese monetary policy was implemented during four specific periods. The PRC used different monetary policy tools to establish various monetary policy targets. During the first period, from 1949 to 1978, the credit plan and the cash plan were used to control the economy. During the second period, from 1978 to 1994, the monetary policy target was the control of inflation and economic growth. The PBC used interest rates and the reserve ratio as monetary policy tools.

Because free movement of foreign currency was forbidden and exchange rates were set by the central bank, maintenance of exchange rate stability was not the monetary policy target before 1994. During the third period, from 1994 to 1998, exchange rate restrictions were removed, but during this period loan ceilings still existed. The maintenance of a stable exchange rate became one of the monetary policy targets.

Open market operation was tested briefly as a monetary policy tool by the PBC in 1995. The results of the tests were inconclusive because of the immaturity of the inter-bank lending market and the treasury bill market. During the fourth period, from 1998 to 2001, the loan ceilings for commercial banks were removed. Prior to 1998 the central bank used loan ceilings to control lending by commercial banks. Since loan ceilings were not used to control commercial banks any longer, the central bank depended on open market operations to control commercial banks indirectly.

The study also discusses the challenges that Chinese banks will face after China joins the World Trade Organization. These challenges include financial risks, the default loan issue, and the bankruptcy issue. The Chinese banking reforms seem to be at an 'optimum order' in the establishment of the banking system, development of the money market, and conduct of monetary policy associated with the fiscal policies and legislation.

It is hoped that this study of China's banking reforms and monetary policy might provide an example for central banking reform in both developing countries and developed countries, should they consider revision of monetary policy.

Yong Guo

Gatlantis International
PO Box 393
Lake Hopatcong, 07849
New Jersey, USA
Phone: (917) 742-2344
email: Gatlantis@Lycos.com

Acknowledgements

I started to prepare this book in 1996 when I was taking economic courses under a fellowship provided by the University of Chicago. Dr David B. Mustard at the Department of Economics, who taught intermediate microeconomics, was very interested in the relative economic systems of China and the United States. Dr Uzma Qureshi, who taught a macroeconomic course, provided me with valuable opinions about inflation and methods to defeat it.

I began to collect Chinese economic data for this book while at Chicago. Mr Luis Garicano shared his studies on information economics. In Dr Gary Becker's microeconomics graduate class, I was enlightened by his statement that 'An important step in extending the traditional theory of individual rational choice to analyse social issues beyond those usually considered by economists is to incorporate into the theory a much richer class of attitudes, preferences, and calculation.' For family reasons I went to New York in 1997. Dr Mustard and Dr Qureshi wrote recommendation letters for me. Dr Janusz A. Ordover and Ms Marge Lesser at New York University approved my application so I became a graduate student under the supervision of Professor Bruce M. Skoorka at the Department of Economics, Leonard N. Stern School of Business, New York University.

When I wrote my graduate thesis, *Banking Reforms in the People's Republic of China and Monetary Policy*, I was actually writing several core parts of this book. My supervisor Mr Skoorka gave me great help. He reviewed, edited and restructured the thesis. He analysed the regression model and the data I collected for the model.

Then I expanded the thesis dramatically to form this book. During this period, several professors at New York University contributed significantly to this book. Mr Steinburg shared with me his financial industry experience on forecasting exchange rates. Mr Janusz Ordover reviewed my work and presented excellent comments on international trade. Mr Dick Netzer at the Robert F. Wagner Graduate School of Public Services of New York University encouraged me greatly in my research and presented to me his research data on tax policy and national assistance to urban areas in the United States.

My research has also benefited from attending seminars hosted by the C. V. Starr Center for Applied Economics (directed by Mr William J.

Baumol). Some data were provided by the People's Bank of China directly. Mr Alan S. Blinder at Princeton University discussed with me in a seminar at the Leonard N. Stern School of Business in 2000 and this book benefits from his thoughts on the central banking systems and monetary policies in both the United States and China.

Dr Jack Michalka kindly spent a lot of time on the word editing of this book and provided many stylistic improvements. Dr Yonglin Ren at First Union and Professor David B. Mustard, now at University of Georgia, provided good suggestions. I would also like to express my deep gratitude to the following in the United Kingdom: Caitlin Cornish, Editor at Palgrave Macmillan Publishing, whose interest in the proposal and manuscript made possible the book's appearance in print; Keith Povey and Anstice Hughes, of Keith Povey Editorial Services, who diligently produced the book and made many extremely useful additional stylistic suggestions. Francis T. Taracido helped in proof-reading.

The University of Chicago provided me with a fellowship in 1995–7 so that I could come to the United States to study economics and gain knowledge of the central banking system of the United States. Dr Gregory D. Jefford, Dr Dale Scholer, Ms Laura Wright, Ms Sheila Russell, Ms Catherine Chin-Chance, Dr Jun Tian, Dr Jeffrey Y. Tang, Dr D. Gale Johnson and Dr Stephen Meredith, at the University of Chicago, all gave me support in my research. I also want to say thanks to Tsinghua University, where I got my BSc and MSc degrees, Xi'an Middle School and Shangzhou School.

My wife, Wenjie, my daughter, Jennifer, and my son, Eric, have cheerfully allowed this book to become a member of the family. My father Xiongyi, mother Fene, brother Wei, father-in-law Wucheng Luo and mother-in-law Shiying Su gave me important support during the writing of this book. Their patience and encouragement over the many months of work were truly amazing and vastly appreciated. I also thank my grandmother Guimei Ren for her support.

YONG GUO

Gatlantis International
PO Box 393
Lake Hopatcong, 07849
New Jersey, USA
Phone: (917) 742-2344
email: Gatlantis@Lycos.com

Abbreviations and Acronyms

ABC	Agriculture Bank of China
ACC	The Agriculture Credit Corporation of China
ACFB	Almanac of China's Finance and Banking
ADB	Agriculture Development Bank
BCCI	Bank of Credit and Commerce International
BOC	Bank of China
CITIC	Chinese International Trust and Investment Corporation
China	The People's Republic of China
CPE	centrally planned economy
CPI	Consumer Price Index
FDIC	Federal Deposit Insurance Corporation (US)
Fed	Federal Reserve System in the United States
FOMC	Federal Open Market Committee
GDP	gross domestic product
GITIC	Guangdong International Trust and Investment Corporation
GLS	Generalized Least Squares
IBC	Investment Bank of China
ICBC	Industrial and Commercial Bank of China
IMF	International Monetary Fund
IS-LM	A macroeconomic model developed by Sir John Hicks in 1937 which explains how interest rates and total output produced in the economy are determined, given a fixed price level.
M	Money supply
M0	Currency in circulation
M1	Currency, checking account deposits, and travellers' cheques
M2	M1 plus other assets that have cheque-writing features (money market deposit accounts and money market mutual fund shares) and other assets (small denomination time deposits, savings deposits, overnight repurchase agreements, and overnight Eurodollars)
MOF	Ministry of Finance of the State Council of China
N/A	not applicable
NASDAQ	National Association of Securities Dealers' Automated Quotation System
OLS	Ordinary least squares

PBC	People's Bank of China
PCBC	People's Construction Bank of China
PRC	The People's Republic of China
RMB	Renminbi, Chinese currency
RPI	retail price index
SDB	State Development Bank
SEC	Securities and Exchange Commission
SOE	State-owned enterprise
TIC	trust and investment company
US	United States of America
WTO	World Trade Organization

Introduction

'Presume not that I am the thing I was.'

William Shakespeare, *Henry IV, Part 2*, V. v. 60

This book is meant to serve as an introduction to Chinese central banking reform as well as monetary policy development. It involves the translation of legislation, of central bank regulations, and of policy. It also involves the examination and analysis of economic literature. The decentralization of banking in the People's Republic of China (PRC) was analysed and compared with current economic theories. This book also describes the Chinese banking reforms involving function and monetary policy.

Chinese central banking reforms from 1978 to 2001 are described. The reforms involve the central bank's monetary policy, the implementation of theories of the gradual decentralization of the banking system. This book also includes the changes in monetary policy during decentralization, and how China's economic system is affected by joining the World Trade Organization.

The gradual changes of monetary policy seemed to be positive for China for much of the time between 1978 and 2001. In the early 1980s China separated commercial banking, policy banking and central banking which were combined prior to 1978. The foreign exchange restriction was eased in 1994.

Because the money market was immature, open market operations failed, and the central bank was forced to abandon them. The central bank was forced to use interest rate adjustment, which was successful in dealing with inflation in 1993. In 1994 foreign exchange restrictions were eliminated. The stability of the exchange rate is one of the targets

1

of the monetary policy (H. Wang, 2001), and open market operations became one of the major monetary policy tools. The reserve requirement and discount rate are also monetary policy tools. The use of these tools established stable economic conditions which reduced the impact of the 1997 Asian Financial Crisis.

Background

Theoretical models predict that financial liberalization can promote economic development such as the Asian miracle in the 1980s and early 1990s. Foreign investment, decentralization of the banking systems, and becoming members of the world financial community permitted Asian countries to increase their savings, investments and the productivity of capital.

However, much of the evidence from financial liberalization in both developed and developing countries suggests significant destabilizing consequences, such as became apparent during the 1997 Asian Financial Crisis. China has benefited from financial liberalization and has not been affected by the crisis.

During the past two decades China achieved one of the world's highest and continuous rates of economic growth (Table 1.1). Chinese gross domestic product (GDP) has been growing annually by 6 to 12 per cent for 23 years. Some of the GDP growth may be slightly overestimated, mainly because small-scale industries sometimes only report output data in the current prices that may not always be deflated by the statistical authorities. But there is no question that the growth is extraordinary. This growth rate is twice the GDP growth rate before 1978 in China.

The performance of the Chinese export–import market is even more impressive. In 1978 total import revenue was $10.89 billion, export revenue was $9.75 billion, and the trade deficit was $1.14 billion. In 1999 total import revenue was $165.72 billion, export revenue was $194.93 billion, and the trade surplus was $29.21 billion. In the 1970s, China's exports grew by 3.4 per cent per year after adjustment for the effects of the Organization of Petroleum Exporting Countries' price increases and related across-the-board inflation. The real export growth rate was 14.1 per cent per year during the first ten years of reform and 10 per cent during the second ten years. China ranked twenty-seventh in international trade in 1978 and moved to the ninth in the world today. International trade was 9.8 per cent of GDP in 1978 and increased to 36.4 per cent today. The Chinese economy gradually became part of the international economy. The Asian Financial Crisis of 1997 did not affect the Chinese economy. Even today, when the United States (US) economy is entering a recession and is struggling to break even with real GDP growth after inflation adjustment, China still announced more than 6 per cent GDP growth in 2001. All of these achievements are due largely to the Chinese banking system reforms.

In the period between 1978 and 2001, the PRC began a series of reforms to modernize the banking and financial system, professionalize the process of sound financial intermediation, and implement a sound and credible monetary policy. The reforms were patterned after the financial architecture of the United States and Europe, as codified in the Glass-Steagall Act of 1933 in the United States (US) and the structure

Table 1.1 GDP and consumer price index of the PRC

Year	Nominal GDP (billion Yuan)	Consumer price index (CPI)	Year	Nominal GDP (billion Yuan)	Consumer price index (CPI)
1952	67.9		1977	320.2	
1953	82.4		1978	362.4	100
1954	85.9		1979	403.8	102.0
1955	91.0		1980	451.8	108.1
1956	102.8		1981	486.2	110.7
1957	106.8		1982	530.2	112.8
1958	130.7		1983	595.7	114.5
1959	143.9		1984	720.7	117.7
1960	145.7		1985	898.9	128.1
1961	122.0		1986	1020.2	135.8
1962	114.9		1987	1195.3	145.7
1963	123.3		1988	1492.2	172.7
1964	145.4		1989	1691.9	203.4
1965	171.6		1990	1859.8	207.7
1966	186.8		1991	2166.2	213.7
1967	177.4		1992	2665.2	225.2
1968	172.3		1993	3456.1	254.9
1969	193.8		1994	4667.0	310.2
1970	225.3		1995	5749.5	356.1
1971	242.6		1996	6685.1	377.8
1972	251.8		1997	7314.3	380.8
1973	272.1		1998	7696.7	381.6
1974	279.0		1999	8042.3	382.3
1975	299.7		2000	8940.4	383.8
1976	294.4				

Source: PBC website (2002); *China Statistics Yearbook*, 1998. For CPI data, taking 1978 data as 100.

and function of the Federal Reserve System. These reforms may have placed the PRC on a sound financial footing in the post-reform era and may have helped to protect the Chinese economy from the effects of the recent financial crisis in Asia.

Prior to the reforms, the People's Bank of China (PBC) operated as a monobank, undertaking both the function of accepting savings, directing credit in the economy, and attempting to implement an immature form of central banking by implementing various forms of financial control. All this changed with the implementation of the reforms. The commercial banking and central banking functions were separated; and the PBC became an independent central bank, relatively free from the government's political interference. It is the purpose of this book to translate and analyse these banking reforms, and to assess the effectiveness of the subsequent implementation of monetary policy empirically.

Issues

Much of the literature on the financial reforms in China stressed the introduction of central banking and monetary policy systems of the European Union and the US into China. The monetary policy tools such as central bank's exclusive control over the setting of interest rates, reserve ratio requirements, the creation of an inter-bank money market, and the implementation of open market operations were introduced from them to change the Chinese system.

Analyses of the central banking system by a large number of authors have shown how to implement provisions of the monetary policy in the decentralization of the Chinese banking system. Very few of these works examine the sequence of the use of these monetary policy tools during the decentralization. They did not examine the link between the sequential use of monetary policy tools and the stages of reforms in other sectors such as agriculture and industry.

Rural agriculture reform in 1978 created the need for a sound financial intermediary. This need resulted in the establishment of the Agriculture Bank of China. More commercial banks were needed as economic reform was implemented in other sectors. In the first stage of banking reform, the commercial banking business was separated from the PBC.

The inflation caused by the price reforms of 1985–8 led the administration to alter fiscal policy to deal with the economy. Failure of the new fiscal policy caused the reappearance of inflation in 1993. The overheated economy in 1993 caused the State Council to transfer power to the central bankers to control inflation. The control of interest rates by the central bank was the powerful tool used to control inflation in 1993.

The reform of the Chinese central bank is required by economic reform. The central bank promotes economic reform. It reacts to microeconomic situations in different ways. Gradual microeconomic reform requires a gradual change in the banking system and changes in the function and improvement of the central banking system. This is a dynamic sequence. If a step of the gradual sequence is missed, failure of the reform might result.

Questions

There are some issues involving the banking reforms in China and the monetary policy of the Chinese central bank. This book considers four important questions in analysing the reforms of the Chinese banking system, the establishment of the central bank and the central bank's conduct of monetary policy.

Should money supply or interest rates be used to control GDP growth?

There are always some arguments about the choice of monetary policy tools: money supply or interest rate. Some people prefer money supply as the tool to control GDP growth and others like interest rates. This argument is so important to central bankers and so interesting to economists that Dornbusch (1998) wrote a whole chapter in his book *Macroeconomics* to analyse it by using *IS-LM* curves.

The Chinese central bank has been trying hard to make a wise decision between interest rate and money supply. The choices between interest rate control and money supply control are discussed globally. This study tries to generate a regression model based on Chinese data. The model may be used by governments to establish prudent monetary policy.

Is there a model involving gradual reform which the central bank can follow?

Is there a general sequence of steps or procedures which might be used by developing countries to liberalize the financial systems? The 'sequence' theory of financial liberalization and the concept of the optimum of economic liberalization establish the order in which fiscal, monetary and foreign exchange policies are implemented. A government cannot, and perhaps should not, undertake all liberalizing measures simultaneously. These models may be appropriate for some countries, but do they apply to China?

Why did the Chinese economy suffer from persistent stop–go cycles (Xu, 1998) in the reform period?

Research data (Xu, 1998) showed the alternate appearance of fast GDP Growth and Slow GDP Growth in PRC in 1980s, a phenomenon called the stop–go cycle.

Why did the authorities permit the monetary expansion associated with such cycles? The low interest rates established by the PBC create a large aggregate demand for capital by enterprises, farmers and government agencies. The demand for loans then exceeds the quota established by the PBC even when the PBC knows the quota is insufficient.

After 1978 the government faced a mounting budget deficit. It pressured local branches of the central bank to finance fixed investments using policy loans. Local governments pressed the local branches of the central bank to extend credit beyond quotas. Local governments partially administered the local branches of the central bank and influenced the financing of large policy loans. In order to finance large policy loans (almost 5 per cent of GDP), the central bank obtained funds from the sale of bonds. These funds are impressively large by international standards.

The monetary policy changes caused stop–go cycles in the Chinese economy. Although the Chinese central bank eliminated the loan ceiling on 1 January 1998, the stop–go pattern still exists.

Where are the financial risks hidden in China?

The Chinese economy was not affected by the 1997 Asian Financial Crisis. Is it possible that the Chinese economy will not be influenced by any financial crisis? Where are the potential risks in the Chinese financial system? One place is the default loan risk. In China 80 per cent of the total loans are from financial intermediaries, originally coming from savings deposits, 15 per cent is from enterprise direct-issued corporate bonds and 5 per cent is from foreign investments. Which produces financial risks: loans from financial intermediaries, enterprise direct-issued corporate bonds or foreign investments?

Loan ceilings were eliminated by the Chinese State Council on 1 January 1998. The four state-owned commercial banks, which provide 75 per cent of total banking loans in China, are still controlled by the government. Have the financial risks from overdue loans in the state-owned commercial banks been reduced by elimination of loan ceilings? What could be the chain reactions of potential financial crises in China caused by the financial risks?

Structure

The study proceeds as follows. Chapter 1 discusses the socialist central banking system and monetary policy in the PRC before 1978. Chapter 2 follows and analyses the evolution of Chinese banking system in the banking reform of 1978–92. Chapter 3 outlines the 1993–7 Chinese banking reforms and describes and then analyses the conduct of monetary policy in this period. Then Chapter 4 discusses how these banking reforms helped China to avoid the Asian Financial Crisis in 1997 and also analyses the central banking reforms after 1997. In Chapter 5, challenges that Chinese banks will face after China joins the World Trade Organization (WTO) are discussed. These challenges include financial risks, the default loan issue and the bankruptcy issue. In Chapter 6 an empirical study is undertaken assessing the effectiveness of the conduct of monetary policy by the PBC in the post-reform era. The empirical model is based on a model originally developed by Poole (1970). Finally, Chapter 7 presents conclusions and suggestions.

Several important conclusions are presented. The Chinese banking reforms seem to be using correct monetary policies and are at least partially responsible for the financial stability in China in the post-reform era. Hence William Shakespeare's 'Presume not that I am the thing I was' (*Henry IV, Part 2*, V. v. 60) describes the change in China. The modernization of the system of financial intermediation, and the strengthening of the central bank's role in regulation and supervision created strong internal conditions for investment. These conditions were based on sound financial principles.

Banking reforms should facilitate internal growth and development, and help to integrate China into the world financial system. The reforms resulting in positive economic growth, will help to prepare China to improve after joining the WTO. Moreover, the results of the empirical study show that the monetary policy in China is appropriate and effective in the post-reform era. Chinese experience of reforms of the banking system seems to suggest the 'optimum order' theory (McKinnon 1993) on financial liberalization.

It is to be hoped that this study of China's banking reforms and monetary policy might contribute to central banking reforms in both developing countries and developed countries, should they consider revision of monetary policy.

1
Socialist Central Banking and Monetary Policy in the PRC

'There are more things in heaven and earth, Horatio,
Than are dreamt of in your philosophy.'

William Shakespeare, *Hamlet*, I. v. 166

1.1 Introduction

The banking sector in the PRC had its beginnings in 1948 with the creation of the PBC, close to the end of the communist revolution. The bank was originally formed by merging three regional banks formerly controlled by the communists under the previous nationalist regime of Jiang Kai-shek: Northern Bank, North Ocean Bank and the Northwestern Agriculture Bank. In 1949 the Bank of China was formed as a spin-off from the People's Bank of China monobank and made responsible for foreign investment, currency exchange and exchange rate policy. In 1952 the Bank of Communications was made responsible to the Ministry of Finance (MOF), and acted as the government's treasury agency for allocating capital investments in the economy. In 1954 the bank was replaced by the newly created People's Construction Bank of China (PCBC), which was in fact the cashier of the Capital Construction Finance Department of the Ministry of Finance in the State Council.

The Chinese banking system was built by learning from the former Soviet Union's centrally planned economy. The principle of the centrally planned economy is that the public owns all the means of production, and that there is no private ownership. Following this socialist rule, the Chinese government spent three years restructuring the private commercial banks and other financial institutions left by the Jiang Kai-shek regime. The government shares were added to the private banks between 1952 and 1955. A new type of bank was created in the commercial banking sector, called state-private corporate banks. Then during the First Five-Year National Plan, that is, between 1955 and 1959, PBC gradually gained total control of the state-private corporate banks and the private shares gradually decreased and finally diminished. Another state bank, the Agriculture Bank of China, came into existence three times, in 1951, 1955 and 1963, under the direction of the PBC. It ceased operation each time shortly after its establishment. The business of the Agriculture Bank of China was handed over to the Bureau of Rural Financial Management inside the PBC. The financial sector established a vertical hierarchy management system. The PBC is the sole root of the banking hierarchy. All the other banks became branches of the PBC. This is the beginning of the monobank in China.

According to Yang (1996), the centrally planned economy (CPE) has the following disadvantages: *(a)* a lack of distinction between the responsibilities of the central administration and those of enterprises; *(b)* bureaucratic inflexibility in the management of enterprises and consequent lack of risk taking and competition at the enterprise level; *(c)* neglect of price indicators through suppression of the market mechanism; *(d)* lack of communication and often distortion of information between different geographical and industrial sectors of production; and *(e)* lack of incentives due to the rigid principle of distributional equality, which could lead to economic inefficiency or low output.

The central banking system in China before 1978

From 1954 to 1978 virtually all financial operations in China were undertaken by a single bank – the PBC. All deposits from individuals and enterprises (almost all enterprises were owned by the state directly or indirectly before 1978) had to be held in accounts with the PBC. Credit could only be obtained there. All business transactions between enterprises had to be settled through the PBC according to the state plan. The payment of salaries could only be made through a separate 'wage fund' account, the quota of which was stipulated by the State Plan and the withdrawal of cash from that account was under the supervision of the bank. The basic framework of the financial system before 1979 is as shown in Figure 1.1.

In that system the PBC was not a traditional commercial bank, nor a central bank. It acted as the government's receiver of money and as the cashier of the State Council. It was the agent of administration of the central plans, which were divided into the credit and the cash plans.

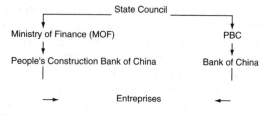

Figure 1.1   Financial structure of the PRC, 1949–78

The PBC was a monopoly bank (monobank) that had sole responsibility for accepting savings deposits from citizens, commercial enterprises and the government, and disseminating industrial and commercial credit in the form of government-directed loans. The bank also served as the sole network for the distribution of currency, and the formulation and conduct of monetary policy.

The transition process to the nationalized monobank system took several years. During the transition, state-private corporate banks gradually changed to branches of the monobank through the PBC's acquisition. By 1955 all the state-private corporate banks were consolidated with the PBC system. Private banking did not re-emerge in China until the 1980s, after the implementation of the 1978 economic reforms under the leadership of Deng Xiao-ping. From 1954 to 1978 the MOF and State Planning Commission managed the economy by a credit planning system called 'Tong Shou Tong Zhi' which means that all financial transactions in China were conducted through the People's Bank of China monobank. Almost all deposits, whether private, commercial enterprise or state, had to be maintained with the PBC, and all business transactions between commercial enterprises had to be settled through the bank. The only bypass existing between 1949 and 1958 was the special credit allocation for rural development. Then in the following twenty years of disruption, mainly during the cultural revolution, the credit allocation for rural development stopped.

1.2   The State Plan system, credit plan and cash plan

The monobank system allowed the Chinese government to establish the State Plan. All credit and investment in China was allocated by the government through the monobank in accordance with the state's One Year Plan, which is the Chinese equivalent of the US Government's Fiscal Budget for a given year. The central bank was under the management of MOF. The central government officials, especially those from the State Planning Commission, decided the state projects, and MOF managed the budget balance by telling the PBC to allocate bank credit to the projects.

Bank credit here has the following characteristics according to Yang's(1996) description:

1. The total amount of the bank credits in the state were calculated according to the fund and resource allocations of the state;
2. Bank credits were allocated directly to projects inside the state-owned enterprises;
3. When mature, defined by the bank according to the production turnover, the fund of credit was repaid by the state-owned enterprises to the bank;
4. All credits were combined with collateral of the enterprises, except new construction projects approved by the state or local governments;
5. A finance charge was made according to additional credit needs, and the state decided the so called 'interest rate', which was not a real interest rate of the traditional commercial banks, and was nothing more than a number convenient to the bank.

The money supply in the PRC before 1978 was segmented into two types of money: cash money and transaction money. Similar to the typical centrally planned economy system in the former Soviet Union, the Chinese state credits linked the government and the public. The government acted as the debtor and the general public as the creditor. The government, through PBC, controlled the economy by separating economic transactions into two types, production transaction and consumption transaction, and had created a different type of money for each kind of transaction: transaction money and cash money. Both came from public savings deposits and from the sale of government bonds.

Cash money was used for income and consumption purposes, and was restricted for use by the household sector of the economy.

Transaction money was used for all inter-enterprise and intra-government transactions, and it was restricted for use by the non-household sector of the economy. Transaction money was not physical money, but accounting money, which existed only on the books of the PBC in the individual accounts of state-owned enterprises and government departments. These booked bank deposits were used to settle transactions between industrial enterprises and government departments, among banks themselves and between the government and quasi-private sector. Monetary policy had to be conducted through these two separate money channels.

From 1950 to 1978, PBC had been using the 'comprehensive credit plans of the state banks' that had the credit plan balance sheet with instructions to the PBC, the specialized banks and the commercial banks. The objective of this credit plan relating to the 'transfer' channel had concentrated on maintaining a level of capital and credit in the banking system consistent with the State Plan for state-directed production and capital investment. These plans were based on the state policies, the State Plans, the current economic conditions and previously tested ways (Yang, 1996).

When the credit plans began to be executed, the PBC had to provide credits to finance the plans and provide funds for the enterprises, the majority of which were state-owned enterprises. The fund had to be raised by the state-owned financial system including branches of the PBC. The PBC set the production targets which required each branch to collect a certain amount of deposit each year. The PBC also required the local branches to allocate the 'transfer' money, on terms set by the central government, to the sectors and enterprises designate. Such direct intervention aimed at inducing priority production and investment, not only in the state sector under central control but also in the non-state sector, such as agriculture, in order to minimize reliance on imports. Production and capital investment targets were formulated in the government's State Plan, and the necessary capital and credit allocation was specified in the credit plan, which was supervised by the State Council and the State Planning Commission (Yang, 1996).

How the credit plan works in industry

The centrally directed industrialization in the PRC before 1978 had common points with the former Soviet Union. Managers focused on quantitative targets, especially those concerning physical output volume and total output value, rather than financial objectives. Profitability did not influence the incomes of executives and workers or the growth prospects of the firms.

The monetary policy process related to the credit-plan 'transfer' channel was more elaborate than the monetary policy process related to the 'cash' channel. The 'transfer' channel was a two-stage process: a top-to-bottom process followed by a bottom-up one. Initially the State Council set the credit plan: a target for the transfer money supply as a function of the planned growth in output and prices, taking into account projected trends in money velocity. The credit plan was then transmitted to the operational section of the bank, which implemented the credit plan. They did this by manipulating the asset side (quota for new loans) and the liabilities side (targets for deposits) of the bank's balance sheet to extend capital and credit where needed.

The bottom-up phase then began. The basic principles of the bottom-up phase followed the rule that quantities of credit were based on the amount of total deposits at the local branches. Provincial branches of the PBC put together their provincial forecasts for deposits and loans expected over the coming year. (These provincial branches have now been replaced by smaller regional commercial banks, which were spun off from the PBC after reforms.) The PBC then revised its initial credit plan in the light of this feedback from its provincial branches (local commercial banks), and the final credit plan was officially approved by the State Council. The State Council then set annual credit ceilings (ceilings for the total amount of loans they could make during the coming year) for the provincial branches of PBC, which then distributed the credit to their local branches. In addition, the State Council set specific credit ceilings on long-term loans (five to ten years) for fixed-capital construction (so-called fixed-asset investment). These long-term loans were allocated to the specific big projects at particular state-owned enterprises. On an annual basis, the commercial banks granted short-term loans (up to one year), called working capital loans, to broad industrial sectors (such as coal-mining). They also made intermediate-term loans (up to five years), called technical innovation loans, to finance equipment purchases by individual state-owned enterprises. The loan ceilings allocated to the local offices of the PBC by the PBC headquarter were based on the branches' savings deposit base.

The negative side

The passive nature of the banking system was further reflected in its role as merely a cashier for the government. It had no role to play in financing long-term investment of the economy because fixed investment funds were allocated entirely through the government budget, free of charge. The mobilization of savings deposits was mainly for the purpose of absorbing excess money from circulation so as to avoid inflation, rather than for increasing investment. The free use of funds led enterprises to involve moral hazard management (page 105). In addition the pre-1979 banking system was almost completely isolated from the outside world and international financial markets. Thus, the banking system had little impact on resource allocation in the economy (Xu, 1998).

The positive side

Chinese industries also had some characteristics different from that of the former Soviet Union. The studies by Yang (1996) showed that China's central plan system was not as tightly controlled in every corner of the industry. As much as 64 per cent of cement, 41 per cent of coal and 23 per cent of the steel industry were allocated outside the central plan system in 1979. The positive outcome of these distinctions was that it gave some power to the managers of the enterprises, local governments and local PBC branches. During the 30 years of the pre-reform period, it prepared enough personnel who are familiar with the so-called 'commerce economy' before the 'market' concept was officially accepted by the Chinese government, as Jiang Ze-min, President of the PRC, stated in the First Plenary Session of the Fourteenth Communist Party Central Committee: 'A planned economy is not only a feature of socialism. Capitalism also has plans. A market economy is not only a feature of capitalism. Socialism also has markets. Both planning and markets are economic mechanisms' (*People's Daily*, 1992). These personnel were ready to enter the risk-bearing loan business after China implemented the commercial loan reform in the 1980s.

Another distinction of the Chinese industry was that 'the ability of planners to obtain compliance with specific detailed directives had always been limited' by the 'extraordinarily weak planning apparatus' (Naughton, 1994). Especially in the rural township enterprises, which usually were poorly equipped and funded, the central plan system usually did not issue credit by the PBC system. Rather, they were financed by the rural credit corporation that was tightly connected with the local government. Thus the central plan system could not fully control the rural township enterprises in both funding and output.

This lack of control saved some collective-owned (not state-owned) enterprises from the destructive power of the ten-year cultural revolution for the rural areas that covered 95 per cent of Chinese territory and had 80 per cent of the Chinese population. Later, when China initiated the economic reform to partially privatize land, properties and enterprises in the rural areas in 1978, the loosely controlled rural township enterprises developed very quickly. They provided the cash for agriculture to buy fertilizers, finance rural infrastructure buildings and provide machines and tools to the farmers quickly and conveniently. If there had been no rural township enterprises, farmers would have had to wait for the State Plan to inefficiently allocate funds and to arrange state-owned enterprises to produce farming machines and tools. It would have meant at least a few years delay of the rural reforms. The rural township enterprises were not starting from nothing when the agriculture reform began in 1978, partly thanks to the loosely controlled characteristics of the Chinese central plan system in contrast to the tightly controlled Soviet Union plan.

The cash plan

The objective of Chinese monetary policy relating to the 'cash' channel had therefore concentrated on maintaining a level of cash money in circulation consistent with the government's growth targets for the real economy as specified in the State Plan. This must be achieved through the annual cash plan. This process assumed that there is a stable relationship between the growth rate of cash money in circulation and production of goods and services through retail sales. This approach to monetary control was implicitly based on the quantity theory of money.

Since the government owned 75 per cent of the industrial enterprises in China (data in 1980), more than 90 per cent of workers were theoretically government employees. To pay these workers, the Ministry of Finance collected all the profits from the state-owned industrial enterprises, and after funding government operations, including the military, passed on the remaining revenues to the workers in these industrial enterprises, often having to make up the difference by printing money. The plan for doing this was called the cash plan. Since China is a centrally planned economy, the State Plan determined what was going to be produced, how much was going to be produced, and by which state-owned industrial enterprises. The State Plan therefore needed to allocate resources, including operating funds and credit, to these industrial enterprises. The plan for doing this, as described earlier, was the credit plan. Hence, under the communist system, all credit was government directed. This was based on the philosophy of Chairman Mao Zedong. However, there are other options in running the Chinese economy: 'There are more things in heaven and earth, Horatio, than are dreamt of in your philosophy' (William Shakespeare, *Hamlet* I. V. 166). Even though it has existed in other countries for many years, a system of sound financial intermediation conducted by professional bankers did not emerge in China until the beginning of central banking reforms in 1978.

2
Structural Change of the Banking System in 1978–92

'Men's judgments are a parcel of their fortunes.'

William Shakespeare, *Antony and Cleopatra*, III. xiii. 31

2.1 Introduction: the need to reform the central banking system

Since the Chinese economy was a centrally planned system, economic reform followed the path of decentralization. According to Yusuf (1994):

> decentralization has occurred at three levels. Administrative decentralization has allowed provincial and local authorities substantial latitude in routine decision-making and the conduct of day-to-day government business... Second, fiscal decentralization, introduced by degrees after 1981 partly in response to demands from lower levels of government, enables provinces to retain and allocate more of the tax revenues collected instead of passing them on to the center... Third, industrial policy and supporting investment in infrastructure has been decentralized.

The monobank system in which local branches of the PBC only reported to the PBC headquarters, then to the State Council, obviously restricted administrative decentralization and fiscal decentralization. Local governments need financial intermediaries to conduct investment, allocation of tax revenues to finance local infrastructure, and other more and more complicated government behaviour. When banking reform later separated the commercial banks from the central bank, local governments fully supported the banking reform and largely benefited from owning the shareholding commercial banks such as Guangdong International Trust and Investment Corporation which was partly owned by the local government in the Guangdong province.

On the industry side, when the communists came to power in China in 1949, the private companies and shareholding companies left by the previous Jiang Kai-shek regime were restructured. Government shares were added to private enterprises between 1952 and 1955. A new type of enterprise was the state-private corporation. Then during the First Five-Year National Plan, between 1955 and 1959, the government either gained total control of the state-private corporations by 'the purchase policy' to make them state-owned enterprises (SOEs) or changed the corporations into so-called 'collective' enterprises owned by local governments or units. The private shares gradually diminished and finally disappeared in 1959. From 1959 to 1978 the SOEs played a dominant role in Chinese industry, producing more than 90 per cent of the total industrial product. The SOEs functioned as the passive agents of state economic bureaucracy. Managers had little authority over research and development, product innovation, investment planning, marketing, or even such routine matters as production scheduling, material purchases, wage structures, and freely hiring and firing employees. They all relied on the State Planning Commission in the State Council, and its subordinates inside local government to set the production plan for them and sell the products for them. Even the prices of the products were dictated by the state. There were little incentives, no competition, and no efficiency before the reform. This was very different from the modern industries supported by efficient financial intermediaries in the Western world.

Since the decentralization of industrial policy in the early 1980s, collective and private enterprises developed rapidly (Table 2.1). The output of the collective enterprises was 38 per cent of the total industry output in 1992, compared with 23.6 per cent in 1980. Private and other enterprises produced 6.8 per cent and 7.2 per cent of Chinese industrial output in 1992, respectively, compared with almost nothing in 1980. The annual real growth rate of private companies output was 64.9 per cent. It is much bigger than the 7.8 per cent growth rate of the SOEs. The rapid growth of the enterprises with private ownership and other forms of ownership is closely linked to the increased demand for pricing reforms, banking reforms and public finance reforms.

At the beginning of the economic reform, the PRC government adopted a soft budget constraint (*People's Daily*, 1987). Fixed capital investment in industry grew by more than 30 per cent, making Chinese

Table 2.1 Shares of nominal output in different ownership groups in Chinese industry and their performance, 1980–92

	1980 (%)	1985 (%)	1990 (%)	1992 (%)	*Average annual growth rate of real output (%)*
State-owned	76.0	64.9	54.6	48.4	7.8
Collective	23.6	32.1	35.6	38.0	18.4
Private	0.0	1.9	5.4	6.8	64.9
Other	0.5	1.2	4.4	7.2	37.2
Total	100.0	100.0	100.0	100.0	13.1

Source: *China Statistics Yearbook*, 1993, pp. 409, 413; Jefferson and Rawski, 1994.

growth investment-driven in the 1980s. Sending scholars overseas to learn about high technology and management, and increasing the investment in imports of manufacturing equipment from the Western world, dramatically speeded up technical progress and introduced efficient production practices. In the meantime it increased the demand for introducing the Western model of financial intermediary.

Since investment is the principal determinant of growth, and domestic savings are the main source of finance for capital accumulation, studying the data for Chinese domestic savings helps to explain why reform of the commercial and central banking system was necessary and urgent for China at the beginning of the economic reform.

A study from Yusuf (1994) showed that the major source of savings in China had switched to household savings from the government/enterprise savings. In 1978 government savings were 15.1 per cent and enterprise savings were 17 per cent of GDP. Household savings were only 1.1 per cent of GDP. Since then there has been a complete turnaround. In 1991 government savings dropped to 1.8 per cent of GDP, while household savings had climbed to 18.7 per cent (enterprise savings remained at roughly the same level, 19.9 per cent of GDP) in 1991.

The reasons for the changes are as follows. First, Chinese culture is oriented towards production rather than consumption. Because of risk perception or low time preference, household spending adjusted slowly to the change in income. Hence, the rapid increase of incomes had inevitably led to piling up of savings. Second, from 1949 to 1978, there was no perception of private ownership of capital under the strict socialist rules, and workers' salaries could barely cover living expenses, so there was little money left for savings. Now that the salaries households receive had increased and private companies were allowed to exist, households and enterprises possessed property rights and the incentive to accumulate had been greatly strengthened. The increased private savings created the market demand of seeking high returns of the money. The concept of investment came in, and financial intermediation is highly demanded.

The recent banking reforms initiated in China in 1978 were designed in part to create a sound banking system as required by decentralization. The banking reform was based on efficient credit and capital allocation through financial intermediation.

2.2   Theories and policy implementation

Generally speaking, the financial system has the following functions: providing a medium of exchange; providing a store of value; mobilizing savings from surplus parties and channelling the funds to productive investments; matching the different maturity requirements of savers and investors; transforming and diversifying the risks. Restoring the above functions is the goal of the Chinese financial reform. The first step will be spinning off the PBC's commercial banking business in order to restore the functions of a sound financial system.

The financial system is composed of financial markets (bond and stock markets) and financial intermediaries (banks, insurance companies, pension funds). It channels funds from the parties who have a surplus of funds without productive investment opportunities to other parties who have a shortage of funds but do have profitable investment opportunities which offer the prospect of high returns. In the pre-reform Chinese capital markets, channeling funds by the financial system was blocked because long-term investment was financed from the state budget through the PBC. The fund was directly allocated by the credit plan, and consideration of repayment was largely ignored. In the finance theory, this direct finance channel bears the high transaction cost (the cost paid to make sure the loans are paid back). In China, the cost of administration is high. For supervising the enterprise operations, the Chinese government set up a communist branch committee in the management team of each enterprise. This created inefficient management and can be treated as another type of transaction cost.

Contrary to direct finance, the financial intermediaries can take advantage of economies of scale to lower the transaction costs. By bundling the funds of many investors together, financial intermediaries can increase the size of transactions. And as the size of transactions increases, the cost per dollar investment decreases. Also, by bundling the funds of many investors together, the dollar cost per investor decreases. In addition, financial intermediaries can take advantage of standardization in their operations. For example, once a loan contract is written, it can be used over and over again, thereby reducing the cost per transaction. The initial writing of the contract is a fixed up-front cost, and average fixed costs decrease with volume. Economies of scale, along with experience and professional expertise, help financial intermediaries reduce transaction costs and promote operating efficiency.

Another reason for the necessity of financial intermediaries is that, in financial markets, one party often does not know enough about another party. For example, when a bank gives a loan to a company for investment in production, the bank does not know the project and the borrower as well as the company itself does, and is less well-informed on such topics as investment risk, credit history, and so on. This is the asymmetric information problem: one party often does not know enough about the other party to make accurate decisions. A borrower who takes out a loan usually has better information about the potential returns and risks associated with the investment projects for which the funds are earmarked than the lender does.

Introducing the financial intermediary can solve the asymmetric information problem. A financial intermediary such as a bank becomes an expert in the production of information about firms so that it can sort out good credit risks from bad ones. Then it can acquires funds from depositors and lend them to sound firms. Because the bank is able to lend mostly to sound firms, it is able to earn a higher return on its loans than the interest it has to pay to the depositors. As a result, the bank earns a profit, which allows it to engage in this information production activity.

2.3 Rural reform and the setting-up of the Agriculture Bank of China

Background

The Great Leap Forward in 1958, the three-year famine from 1959 to 1962, and the 'Cultural Revolution' from 1966 to 1976 almost destroyed industry, agriculture and the regular living standard of the Chinese people. In order to survive, normal functioning of economic operations had to be restored. Immediately after taking office, Deng Xiao-ping proposed new legislation and announced plans to begin the economic reform. The official step was the opening of the Third Plenary Session of the Eleventh Communist Party Central Committee in December 1978. It officially ended the Cultural Revolution and initiated the economic reforms.

As an agricultural country, China had the priority to restore the disrupted financial arrangements towards the rural region. The process of reforms first started in agriculture and then extended to industry. Since 1978 agriculture boomed, initially increasing at an annual average rate of 8 per cent from 1979 to 1984.

The rural reforms comprised two related parts. The first was decollectivization. Peasants were allowed to own some land, but were not allowed to sell it. This were called 'the operation rights of land without ownership'. They were allowed to farm the land as a household unit, manage the land at their own risk, and at their own return as well. When they harvested crops, they could keep most of them after selling a certain amount to the government at the state defined prices. Peasants were no longer required to work in the collectives after the 1978 rural reform. The reform broke the inefficient utopian collective system inside which peasants were working together and sharing the products. This change stimulated the peasants' creativities and activities. It increased productivity and produced enough food to support the 800 million rural population.

The second part of the rural reform was the opening of free markets for the peasants to trade agricultural sub-products and commodities, which is agricultural products excluding crops. But trading of major crops was still controlled by the government till 1985 when the State Council allowed trading of major crops in the open market. In the second half of the 1980s, around 60 per cent of agricultural commodities were bought and sold on competitive markets, as compared to only 8 per cent in 1978 (Lu and Timmer, 1992). But the other 40 per cent of major crops were still traded under the government-defined prices. The rural reform gradually increased the free trading portion. By 1990 the percentage of the free traded agriculture products and commodities increased to 80 per cent. By 2001 almost all agriculture prices were freed up. The government uses the state reserve crops to maintain the crop price level at a certain range by trading in when the market price drops or by sale when the market price rises. The policy of food rationing to urban citizens over the past 40 years is totally abandoned.

The response of agriculture to the rural reforms was quick. From 1978 to 1984 the growth rate for agricultural value added was five times what it had been over the previous two decades. Growth statistics also indicate that the agriculture output spurt was a one-shot affair largely exhausted by the end of 1984, when most crop production returned to its long-term growth rate (Perkins, 1994).

The decollectivization and the freeing up of rural markets both needed financial support. The peasants needed funds to buy fertilizers.

Trading of agricultural commodities required the bank to transfer funds. It was an economic necessity to break the monobank restriction and to create an efficient commercial bank to do business in rural areas. The Agriculture Bank of China was re-established under these circumstances. The Agriculture Bank of China is the first commercial bank established after 1978 (Yusuf, 1994).

The separation of the Agriculture Bank of China from the Central Bank

The Agriculture Bank of China (ABC) was originally established in 1951. Later it was closed and was re-established twice and finally re-established in December of 1978 with the purpose of promoting rural development, an activity that was conducted by a department of PBC before 1978. The ABC's role is to provide working capital to state agricultural supply and marketing units in rural areas. It also grants loans to the township and village enterprises. In return, its deposits come mainly from agricultural supply and marketing units, and individual deposits in rural areas, and since 1990 in urban areas as well. The ABC has 30 provincial-level branch offices, more than 2,000 sub-branches in rural areas and more than 500 offices in the urban areas.

The ABC guaranteed the funds for farmers and peasants to buy fertilizer, seeds and other agricultural necessities. Since the rural and agricultural regions covered 90 per cent of Chinese territories and 80 per cent of the Chinese population, roughly 800 million farmers and peasants back in 1978, the total funds managed by the ABC was huge, totalling 1.57 trillion Yuan RMB in 1997, almost doubling in the five years comparing with 1992 (Table 2.2). This fund has been managed by the Rural Financial Management Bureau of PBC since 1955. In 1978 it was handed over to the ABC.

The re-establishment of the ABC showed that the Chinese hoped to manage rural financial business in a professional way by banks. The ABC supported rural business and agriculture mainly through short-term and long-term loans (long-term loan did not show up in the balance sheet until 1995). Both loans grew steadily at an average annual growth rate of 19–30 per cent most of the time. The only exception happened in 1995 when the short-term loan increased by only 3.8 per cent. The reason was that some of the short-term loans were switched to long-term loans in that year because of starting long-term loans for the first time. If both long-term and short-term loans were added together in 1995, the total number would be 690.155, a 16.7 per cent increase (Table 2.2).

From this starting point, the Chinese made a series of reforms to modernize the banking system in the following two decades.

Table 2.2 Balance sheet of the Agriculture Bank of China (Billion Yuan RMB)

	1991	1992	1993	1994	1995	1996	1997
Asset							
Short loan	457.8	546.8	652.9	591.148	614.826	802.190	918.270
Long-term loan					75.329	96.320	99.947
(– 'bad' loan)					(4.318)	(4.191)	(3.992)
Foreign exchange	17.2	27.3	38.0	29.678			
Credit & investment	12.1	25.0	27.0	17.996			
Brokerage	9.4	9.9	10.9				
Broker for agricultural development Bank				287.893			
Cash	7.1	8.8	13.4	15.18	15.921	13.535	15.489
Saving in the central bank	42.8	34.1	53.4	57.036	182.268	241.161	251.835
Policy saving in the central bank				7.927			
Reserve	43.1	51.8	63.7	86.207			
Lend other banks	27.8	57.8	39.5	65.133	57.666	61.139	39.056
Short-term borrowing between banks					46.664	57.707	41.166
Buy bond(long investment)	6.1	8.0	10.3		36.396	43.519	40.123
Short-term investment					11.432	19.287	12.821
Capital	7.2	7.8	21.0	25.036	194.767	136.28	159.232
Other capital	56.2	90.8	126.4	38.869			
TOTAL	686.8	868.1	1056.5	1253.053	1230.951	1466.947	1573.947

24

Table 2.2 (continued)

	1991	1992	1993	1994	1995	1996	1997
Liability							
Savings	331.9	413.1	518.4	633.802	737.954	962.340	1143.807
Foreign exchange	14.7	23.4	35.8				
Credit & investment debt	12.1	25.1	27.0	164.384			
Brokerage	9.6	10.1	11.1	196.65			
Loan from central bank	175.0	208.1	278.5	84.748	86.942	267.509	205.594
Saving from other banks	30.1	45.7	31.9	54.584	220.781	75.426	72.078
Short-term borrowing between banks	20.812	20.552	9.504				
Issuing bonds	1.5	1.9	1.0				
Other	79.6	106.2	121.2	251.07	123.684	98.962	103.195
Capital	32.3	34.5	31.6	44.8	40.778	42.158	39.760
TOTAL	686.8	868.1	1056.5	1253.053	1230.951	1466.947	1573.947

Source: ACFB, 1998.

2.4 Building a commercial banking system

In the first phase of banking reform, commercial banks were separated from the central bank. After the ABC was re-established in 1978, the Bank of China (BOC) was spun off from the PBC to conduct the foreign exchange business.

Before 1978 China's centrally planned system did not allow free trade between domestic enterprises and foreign markets. According to Perkins (1994), 'There was an "air lock" between all producing enterprises and world markets so that prices on world markets had no influence on the domestic price structure'. Should the enterprises need foreign currency to import foreign goods, they had to apply to the PBC to allocate funds for them. The exchange rate was defined manually by the PBC, not according to the long-term equilibrium market value of the currency. The reforms of 1978 allowed enterprises for the first time to buy imported machines and materials directly. It stimulated the enthusiasm of enterprises to buy foreign products. This caused a shortage of foreign currency holding. The previously mandated exchange rates needed to be re-adjusted. In 1979 the new wave of reforms introduced to facilitate exports of manufactures and allow for foreign investment increased the urgency of making exchange rate re-adjustment.

In response to the increased need for financial arrangements on the foreign trade and exchange rate policy-making during the reform, the Bank of China (BOC) was spun off from the PBC in March 1979. It finally became independent from the PBC and specialized its business in foreign exchange in September 1983. Since its inception the exchange rate changed from 1.7 Yuan to the US dollar in 1981, to 2.9 Yuan to the US dollar in 1985, to 4.8 Yuan to the dollar in 1990, and finally to about 8.29 Yuan to the dollar in 2002. The BOC served as an import–export bank, implemented exchange controls and regulations and managed all exchange-related transactions and operations in the country. It is currently under the supervision of the PBC and works closely with the PBC in maintaining the country's exchange stability.

The Investment Bank of China (IBC) was established in December 1981. It collects funds abroad and undertakes investment business.

The People's Construction Bank of China (PCBC) was created in 1954 under the direct leadership of Ministry of Finance (MOF). It distributed budgetary appropriations to SOEs, provides funds for the expansion of existing enterprises, and supervises the use of those funds. After 1979 the cost-free funds issued by PCBC were replaced by loans. In January 1983 the PCBC officially changed its former function of acting as a government agency. It was made to integrate into the banking system. Its business is now supervised by the PBC.

The commercial banking side of the PBC was transferred to the Industrial and Commercial Bank of China (ICBC) that opened in January 1984 to handle the business of urban savings deposits, loans for working capital and medium-term credits for equipment purchases of enterprises, which was one of the functions of the PBC before. Since its establishment, the ICBC had been the largest bank in China both in terms of its assets, which accounted for about 31 per cent of the combined banking assets in 1992, and in terms of its domestic business operations, which accounted for 47 per cent of the total business operations of the so-called specialized banks (a term used by Chinese government to include all commercial banks owned by the Chinese government and other private and shareholding commercial banks) excluding the BOC (World Bank, 1993). In addition ICBC, with a large countrywide network of more than 30,000 branches, also engaged in trust business, either directly or indirectly through its trust and investment company (TIC) affiliates.

Here the ICBC balance sheet can be used as an example to analyse the typical state-owned commercial banks in China, as shown in Table 2.3. On the asset side, the brokerage business ceased in 1994 and credit/investment business ceased in 1996, reflecting the legislation of separation of commercial banks from the investment banking business, which will be discussed in later chapters. Foreign exchange business stopped in 1994. It reflects the PBC control of the foreign exchange rate of RMB. The short-term borrowing from the inter-bank lending market began to show up in the balance sheet in 1995. The PBC's first attempt at open market operation was also in 1995. The PBC was trying to develop the inter-bank lending market for its monetary policy implementation. However, the volume of inter-bank lending dropped through 1997 to 14.834 billion Yuan (Table 2.3). It shows that banks are reluctant to borrow from inter-bank lending because of the high interest rate. The 'bad' loan for the first time showed up in the commercial banks' balance sheets in 1995. This is the start of PBC's financial supervision for defaulted loans, the details of which will be fully discussed in the later chapters.

These four newly created mission-oriented commercial banks managed more than 90 per cent of the total banking assets in China. These banks, although still state owned, were required to conduct bank operations in a manner that embodied the principles of professional financial intermediation, including the assessment of credit risk in making

Table 2.3 Balance sheet of the Industrial and Commercial Bank of China (billion Yuan)

	1989	1990	1991	1992	1993	1994	1995	1996	1997
Asset									
Loan	575.19	687.19	797.120	933.709	1112.823	1276.809	1481.104	1800.071	1995.056
(−) 'bad' loan							(11.269)	(12.576)	(7.856)
Foreign exchange	13.434	21.750	29.716	45.078	81.904				
Credit/investment business	32.000	33.600	42.265	59.200	81.604	93.552	59.792		
Brokerage business	51.028	59.027	68.561	65.358	69.823				
Cash	4.710	5.244	5.696	9.658	17.409		367.559	453.854	502.736
Saving in central bank	17.421	35.769	53.720	30.989	59.892				
Reserve	52.478	66.143	83.059	100.796	118.172		30.967	23.866	16.873
Short-term borrowing between banks									
Lend to other banks	2.612	4.305	2.886	6.433	28.385	60.588	976.897	1026.210	1209.567
Buying T-bond	7.358	10.247	13.492	18.941	23.574		87.456	113.029	117.883
Net capital	6.486	7.951	10.170	12.977	17.518	18.750	26.753	38.164	40.022
Other capital	9.818	7.142	10.784	150.514	347.954	58.831	88.237	186.952	174.641
TOTAL	772.535	938.368	1117.469	1433.653	1959.058	2633.938	3107.496	3629.570	4048.922

Table 2.3 (continued)

	1989	1990	1991	1992	1993	1994	1995	1996	1997
Liability									
Savings	413.109	5173.49	640.503	796.23	884.444	1191.019	1512.737	1900.885	2251.050
From enterprises	183.112	223.039	277.386	365.064	362.881	646.011			
From citizens	229.997	294.310	363.117	431.166	521.563	545.008			
Foreign currency Exchange	13.118	21.203	28.910	34.937	71.373				
Credit & investment business	27.690	29.290	36.986	51.559	71.100	83.651	54.150		
Brokerage	52.390	62.129	71.524	65.711	713.44				
Borrowed from central bank	173.654	202.436	217.825	239.512	351.412	279.888	263.829	231.305	178.012
Short-term borrowing between banks							13.976	18.539	14.834
Savings from other banks	3.174	3.785	1.475	2.606	60.309		973.695	1093.269	1268.558
Issuing bonds	2.464	3.239	6.357	9.513	7.220	5.694	5.568	5.721	0.991
Other	36.380	43.617	49.901	163.139	353.885	174.724	190.830	285.697	238.621
Capital	50.556	55.32	63.988	70.446	87.971	87.664			
TOTAL	772.535	938.368	1117.469	1433.653	1959.058	2633.938	3107.496	3629.570	4048.922

Source: ACFB, 1998.

loans to qualified industrial enterprises for viable projects, and making a profit in the process. These banks were not to be subsidized by the State Council. Issuing bonds was permitted by the PBC to raise funds for commercial banks in 1985. Total domestic bonds raised funds of 9.2 billion Yuan RMB in 1988–9. Although a large portion of the bank's savings deposits were earmarked by the government for state-directed loans, a significant portion of the bank's deposits could now be used to make loans and investments deemed safe and profitable to the bank. This served to partially liberalize the banking sector. Banks could now begin to engage in some professional banking activity in a manner consistent with the professional banking practices common in the developed countries.

In addition, the newly spun-off commercial banks were required to hold a fraction (13 per cent in 1979) of their total assets in the form of cash reserves with the PBC. Although not a true fractional reserve banking system, the PBC could use this arrangement to regulate the level of credit in the banking system by manipulating the discount rate and controlling the level of commercial bank borrowing. Figure 2.1 shows the banking structure in China after 1978.

Figure 2.1 shows the rapid development of city commercial banks and urban credit corporations such as Fujian Industrial Bank and Shenzhen Merchants Bank since the banking reform started in 1978. At the end of 1998 China had 88 city commercial banks, 3200 urban credit corporations, and 50,000 rural credit corporations. Their assets were 2.1 trillion Yuan RMB in 1998, and these assets were 16.4 per cent of all commercial banking assets in China (*China Statistics Yearbook*, 1999).

A total of 609.1 billion Yuan RMB was deposited in city commercial banks and urban credit corporations in 2000. They granted loans of 388.3 billion Yuan RMB that represented an average annual increase of 56 per cent in 2000 when compared with loans granted the previous year. Eighty per cent of the loans were granted to private companies and small- and middle-sized urban collective enterprises (*China Statistics Yearbook*, 2000, 2001).

The rural credit corporations have also developed rapidly since 1978 (Figure 2.1). The rural credit corporations serve both the rural and urban populations, and support private companies and small enterprises. They create employment opportunities, support local developments and increase state income. They stimulate reforms of state-owned commercial banks, and they have established an environment for Chinese commercial banking reform. They operate using the same rules that are used by commercial banks, and their employees are efficiently managed and knowledgeable. The presence of rural credit corporations allows the four state-owned commercial banks to focus on serving big enterprises in large

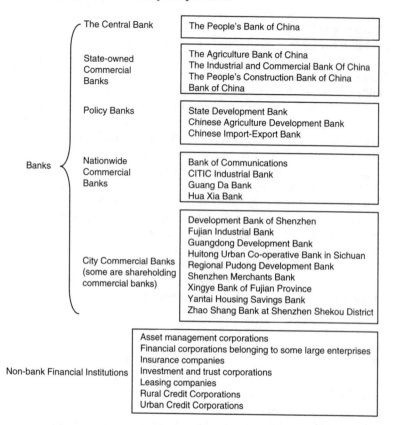

Figure 2.1 The structure of the financial system in the PRC after 1978
Source: People's Bank of China; *ACFB* (1999); *China Statistics Yearbook* (1999).

cities and makes it possible for small enterprises and other types of companies to receive better services from private financial corporations.

By 2000 the rural credit corporations had total deposits of 1219 billion Yuan RMB and granted loans of 834 billion Yuan RMB. When compared with the figures for 1986, the average annual increases between 1996 and 2000 were approximately 24 per cent for both savings and loans (*China Statistics Yearbook*, 2001). Agriculture, rural collective enterprises, home businesses and farmers received 80 per cent of the loans from the rural credit corporations.

Shareholding banks in China

In addition to the four state-owned commercial banks, which managed 87 per cent of the total financial assets in China, there are some shareholding banks such as the Bank of Communication, which was restructured in 1986, and CITIC (Chinese International Trust and Investment Corporation) Industrial Bank (established in 1987 as a full subsidiary of the CITIC). Both of them position themselves as more commercially oriented banks. Similarly, many other banks were established: the Xingye Bank of Fujian Province (in November 1981), the Huitong Urban Co-operative Bank in Sichuan Province (in February 1985), the Zhao Shang Bank at Shenzhen Shekou district (in August 1986), the Development Bank of Shen Zhen City (in June 1987) and the Development Bank of Guangdong Province (in June 1988). Unlike the four state-owned commercial banks, these banks are owned by the shareholders, usually big enterprises, local governments, or private companies, and managed by the board of major shareholders.

Shareholding banks have been in the Chinese financial markets for some years. There are always some arguments about the state-owned commercial banks and the shareholding banks. Should the central bank change the rules so that state-owned commercial banks could become shareholder owned? In doing so, the state can become the biggest shareholder of the commercial banks. The commercial banks will then be responsible to the board of directors and the shareholders' meeting. Profit maximization will become the sole target of the commercial banks' business.

Theories: state-owned versus shareholding commercial banks

In order to compare the state-owned commercial banks with the shareholding commercial banks, theories of information economics should be mentioned. As discussed at the beginning of the chapter, under asymmetric information in financial markets, one party often does not know enough about the other party to make accurate decisions. The asymmetric information causes the principal–agent problem. The principles are the people who give away part of their decision-making powers, such as the Chinese government. The Chinese government is the owner of the four state-owned commercial banks. The agent, the managers in the state-owned commercial banks, will probably do whichever is good for the managers or for the commercial bank itself, not for the government's benefits. This inconsistence of interest between the bank owner and the bank manager is an example of the principal–agent problem.

Benefit of the shareholding banks

The shareholding commercial banks break the monopoly of the state-owned commercial banks and establish management systems according to international financial standards. They have a board of directors, shareholder meetings and auditing systems. The ownership of the banks is effectively separated from the operation. The shareholding banks apply banking balance sheet management, risk management and strict standards for granting loans. In the PRC, long before the state-owned commercial banks began to deal with the default loan problem, shareholding banks already practised the writing off of default loans.

The shareholding banks create a competitive environment in the Chinese financial markets. The risk prevention concept is introduced into the Chinese financial markets. All this promotes the state-owned commercial banks' reform of management systems, financial innovation, and marketing practice. It helps to improve the state-owned commercial bank's services and efficiency.

Because of the benefit of reducing the principal–agent problem, the shareholding commercial banks in the PRC have developed very quickly since their inception. There were 110 shareholding commercial banks by 2001. The total assets were 2600 billion Yuan RMB in 2001, which was 19 per cent of the total commercial banking assets in the PRC. Among them were 9 cross country operated shareholding commercial banks with total assets of 1852.5 billion Yuan RMB and 99 local city commercial banks with total shareholding banks assets of $709.6 billion Yuan RMB (Deng, 2001).

According to Deng (2001), the shareholding commercial banks in China have bank capital of 8 per cent. This number is low in terms of risk management, compared with the international banking capital requirement. For example, the Citigroup in the US has 2.74 per cent capital reserves only for preparing the risks such as default loans. Another potential problem in the shareholding commercial banks in China is the increasing level of 'bad' loans. Total 'bad' loan ratio was 16.46 per cent in the 10 shareholding commercial banks and 31.01 per cent in the 99 local city shareholding commercial banks in 2001. In addition, the shareholding commercial banks only have 20 per cent of total Chinese commercial banking assets and are restricted to certain businesses such as deposit-taking, loan-granting and some foreign exchange business. Their investment banking business is restricted.

Proposal for developing shareholding commercial banks in China

There are some proposals for improving the business of the existing shareholding commercial banks. The shareholding commercial banks will reinforce their management structures. The relationships among the board of directors, the shareholder meeting and the auditing system are intended to protect the rights of middle and small shareholders and encourage the creativities of the employee by arranging a proper compensation plan and a stock option plan to prevent the principal–agent problem. The quarterly profit earnings information release rules will be emphasized. In addition, shareholding commercial banks will learn from the foreign commercial banks and take advantage of international financial innovations such as online banking to supplement their inadequate office networks across the country.

There are some proposals suggesting changing the state-owned commercial banks to the shareholding structure: the bank managers will have some stock options, and will be able to own a part of the banks. This will partially solve the principal–agent problem. But China does not have any short-term plan to do this yet.

The financial corporations

In this wave of financial reforms, the non-bank financial institutions also gained the chance of developing. Two types of non-banking financial institutions developed quickly. One is the investment and trust company, some of which belong to banks and others to local companies. The other type is called financial corporations.

A financial corporation is the combination of financial instituions and industry enterprises. In the Western world, financial corporations conduct the business of consumer loans, corporate bonds and investment consulting. They are non-bank financial institutions with the major function of stimulating product sales. For example, in the US, General Electric (GE) has a financial subsidiary called GE Capital. And General Motor (GM) owns GMAC. In China the financial corporations are the dependent companies of the large enterprise groups with the business focus of banking, trust, leasing, investment and stock and bond trading. They first went public in 1984. There were more than 70 financial corporations in China by 1999.

Major characteristics of financial corporations

One of the characteristics of financial corporations is dual representation. Compared with banks, financial corporations belong directly to the parent companies, most of which are manufacturing enterprises. On the other hand, the financial corporations themselves are financial firms. They cover almost all the financial business except insurance, accepting private deposits and making private loans.

Since the financial corporations belong to parent enterprises that are different in business, the financial corporations can hardly share common points with each other. They are different in business type, business range, operation size, profitability and operation purpose.

The financial corporations create profits for the parent enterprises, contribute more than 10 per cent of investment for the parent companies' research and development, provide 15 per cent of short-term loans to the parent companies and provide convenient clearing services between the different departments within the parent enterprise. In 1999, 31 per cent of the profits of the financial corporations in China came from inter-bank loan interest income because inter-bank loans have an interest rate 500 basis points higher than the rate that the enterprise would get from savings (H. Xie, 1999).

In the PRC, the State Council defined the function of the financial corporations as 'help capital flow inside the enterprise that the financial corporation belongs to' in the State Council document [1991, #71]; and reinforced this function again in another State Council document in 1997 [1997, #15]. This definition from the State Council contains no detailed description. It allowed room for the Chinese financial corporations to develop diversified business without violating the law. That is why the financial corporations in China have little in common.

The financial corporations also created a dilemma for the PBC. According to the definition, the financial corporations directly serve the large SOEs and should be supported by the PBC. The PBC can hardly refuse applications to set up new financial corporations. On the other hand, the increasing number of financial corporations intensified the pressure for central bank supervision.

There are some other difficult parts for the PBC to handle. The financial corporations hope to penetrate into both commercial banking and investment banking business due to the large potential profits. The original function of stimulating technology innovation and doing research and development is liable to be overlooked.

All the above difficulties present a dilemma to the PBC. If the PBC agrees to the definition of the function of the financial corporations as 'serve enterprises', there will be more and more financial corporations on the way to be chartered given the large number of large SOEs. (Theoretically, every SOE can apply for setting up a financial corporation.) If the PBC wants to define detailed functions for financial corporations, in order to limit their number, this task is even more difficult for PBC than the task of financial supervision (H. Xie, 1999).

Foreign banks in China

In 1979 China opened six cities for foreign banks to set up branches, but from 1982 this regional restriction was partially abandoned. Twenty-three cities plus Hai Nan province were opened to foreign banks to set up branches. Eight foreign banks, which are Bank of Tokyo/Mitsubishi, the Industry Bank of Japan, Citigroup, Hong Kong Bank, Daiichi Kangyo Bank, Shanghai-Paris International Bank, Standard Chartered Bank and Sanwa Bank were allowed to trade in the Ren Min Bi (RMB) market in 1996 (Lee, 2000). In 1998 the PBC continued to enlarge the range of Chinese currency (RMB) business permitted to foreign banks. Nine more foreign banks were allowed to collect RMB deposits and grant RMB loans in Pu Dong district of Shanghai city. Shengzhen became the second city for the foreign banks to do RMB business. In 1999 the PBC made efforts to amend the regulations for foreign banks doing RMB business, so that foreign banks can set up branches not only in the 23 cities plus Hai Nan province defined in 1996, but also in all the other major cities in China. While increasing the supervision of foreign banks, the PBC lowered the entry standard in order to allow foreign banks to set up local branches more easily.

By 2000 foreign banks had total assets of $34.6 billion US dollars, which was 1–2 per cent of the total commercial banking assets in China.

2.5   Reforms of the banking function

After the spin-off of commercial banks from the PBC, the Chinese government could no longer withdraw funds directly from the monobank. It has to issue treasury bills or government bonds through the central banking system to finance the state budget. On the central bank side, the PBC has some power to conduct certain monetary policies independently. For example, the PBC is given some rights to reject the investment projects from the State Planning Commission at the State Council if the projects violate the rules drawn up by the central bank. The government had to gradually change its financing channels by issuing bonds and treasury bills after 1978. Before 1978 the government usually directly ordered the PBC to withdraw cash to finance the state budget.

On the enterprise side, from 1979, the government stopped granting enterprises capital investment from the cost-free state budget. Instead, they began to collect interest for those loans. In early 1979 the People's Construction Bank of China (PCBC) was re-established and began running a pilot scheme of interest-bearing investment loans. The result turned out to be excellent. The commercial banks' lending for industry fixed capital investment increased to about 80 per cent in 1985 from only a very tiny share of the total capital investment in 1979 (World Bank, 1988).

Under the 1979 reforms the Chinese government began to decentralize the process of deposit taking and lending to the local branches of the PBC. The commercial bank reform target is the so-called 'enterprising of the specialized banks', meaning that the banks doing the commercial banking business should be specialized to be responsible for the profits and losses as an enterprise. They will be just like the commercial banks in the Western world. This was intended to allow local bankers to learn and use professional banking skills and facilitate a true process of sound financial intermediation in the Chinese banking system. The reforms were codified in a memorandum issued by the State Council in April 1979, called the 'Memorandum of the National Meeting of the Local Branch Heads of the People's Bank of China.' The new approach was called the 'Unified Plan'. It required the local branch heads to establish a link between deposits and loans consistent with a target 'gap' between the level of loans and the level of deposits. It was established by the state in the annual credit plan.

According to this document, bank credit funds were to be managed in the new method of control under 'unified plans', administered at different levels, with 'the establishment of a link between deposits and loans, and control over differences between bank loans and bank deposits' (Wu, 1995). Thus, the head office of the PBC would, according to the state-approved credit plan, assign the target amount of the annual difference (gap) between credits and deposits at its provincial level branches. Then it could establish control over 'the difference between bank loans and bank deposits'. Deposits were administratively transferred from branches with a positive gap to branches with a negative gap, through the head office of the PBC. The essence of the more deposits/more lending policy, begun in the second half of 1979, consisted of encouraging banks to collect more deposits by granting them the rights to extend more loans, as long as they respected a planned gap between deposits and loans. This policy was effective between 1979 and 1988.

According to Yang (1996), the gap-transfer system did not ensure PBC control over the overall volume of credit or aggregate money supply. The main reason behind this difficulty lies in the asymmetry inherent in such a system. The head office was obliged to transfer funds automatically to the local branches having a negative gap, but branches with a planned positive gap could very well have a much greater excess of deposits over loans than planned. Hence, *ex post* credit expansion could well turn out to be greater than planned, since the shortfall in deposits with these positive-gap branches could be noticed by the head office only when it had happened.

To further analyse financial development in China some indicators were introduced. Xu (1998) studied the M1/GDP values from 1979 to 1990 in China. From McKinnon (1973, 1993)'s idea of using M2/GNP to show the degree of financial liberalization, Xu defined M1/GDP as the financial depth of the Chinese economy. The number shows the regular pattern of fluctuation. This is consistent with the famous 'stop–go model' in the Chinese post-reform economy. In February 1981 the 'control over the differences between loans and deposits' was changed to 'the contract responsibility system for an agreed amount on the difference between bank lending and bank deposits'. That is, the various branches could extend credit on the basis of the level of deposit so that 'the higher the level of deposit the larger the amount of credit [that] could be extended'. Xu found that in 1982 M1/GDP kept almost unchanged, in other words, the credit expansion decreased due to the policy adjustment.

In 1985 it happened again, but in the direction towards expansion. 'The contract responsibility system' was replaced by the method of 'unified planning, control of bank lending by separate categories, establishing that lending could only be permitted when there was an equivalent actual amount of deposit, and the establishment of inter-bank lending'. The financial depth (M1/GDP) jumped to 0.35 from 0.29 in 1982. This was partly due to the money control loosened by the 1984 separation of the PBC from four specialized state banks – the ICBC, the ABC, the PCBC and the BOC. The separation permitted the four specialized banks to give credits to industry. This separation should have enabled the PBC, which became a proper central bank, to improve its control of credit because each branch of the state banks was obliged to deposit its reserves (required or extra) with the PBC and it had to apply to the central bank when it needed to borrow funds. But it did not prove very effective. As far as the PBC is concerned, there seems to be ample evidence to suggest that serving the Chinese government's economic growth policy has priority over maintaining monetary stability. This growth-oriented policy essentially means that the Chinese government will not tolerate economic and financial adjustments that require prolonged static growth that might threaten to bring about large-scale retrenchment and high unemployment. The banking system is therefore required to ensure funding to maintain the survival of state enterprises and to provide loans according to the government's industry policy. As a result, the old credit plan is still PBC's main weapon to control credit and money supply. Some researchers (Girardin, 1997) found that movements in bank loans come before cash issue, not after. State banks were able to engage in excessive credit creation because the PBC allowed them to exceed their credit ceilings and granted them excessive loans.

In fact the PBC itself seems to have side-stepped the credit plan. It resolved the conflict between the enforcement of credit ceilings and the financing of state banks by granting temporary loans (i.e. seasonal and daily loans). Such loans are supposed to meet the necessary but unpredictable financing needs of specialized banks, so they lie outside the credit plan.

As a rule, at the PBC's interest rates, the aggregate demand for capital by enterprises, farmers and government agencies is usually much larger than the quotas, because the cost of capital is expected to be very low relative to the return on successful investments, and because of the potential for transferring losses to the central government. The policy-makers were aware that the bank quotas under the credit plan would generally have to be exceeded. The PBC even made known the imbalance in the credit plan. In official Chinese terms, the credit plan often had a gap. The gap was usually 10 per cent of the credit plan. When financial intermediaries do not expect an excess supply of funds to finance the quota, at the PBC's interest rates, the excess demand for capital can be eliminated by a combination of four options: reducing the risk borne by lenders; increasing the effective interest rate paid by borrowers; obtaining a larger quota and therefore access to PBC resources; and shifting the excess demand to other sources of financing.

A more detailed exposition of the issue is presented in Leroy Jin's book (1994), which is devoted to an analysis of the most puzzling question of the contemporary period: why has the Chinese economy suffered from persistent stop–go cycles in the reform period, and why have the authorities tolerated the monetary expansion associated with such cycles? Jin begins with a recognition of the fact that the government in China has relied largely on administrative credit controls to implement monetary policy, and so far has not been able to employ instruments to control base money supply. The monetary expansion comes from two sources: (1) the expansion of the share of households in aggregate savings and thus, an expansion of the bank deposits, given a lack of alternative non-money savings instruments, due to the limited development of the securities market. Wu (1995) also indicated the 30 per cent annual increase of the household savings rate; (2) periodic expansions of bank credit, lending largely for investment purposes.

Why did the government tolerate such expansions, in a system where credit allocation was supposedly assigned by bank quotas? According to Girardin (1997), the main mechanism behind this credit expansion has been traced to a game between the state and local governments over the financing of investment in state-owned enterprises. The local branches of the PBC are dependent on local governments. They were vulnerable to pressure from local governments to permit local banks to extend credit beyond the planned ceilings. The local governments tend to lack any incentive to make infrastructure investment and investment for the technical updating of SOEs. By contrast, the central government wants investment resources to flow to strategic sectors such as energy and raw materials and then has to take full responsibility for financing these SOEs. As the government was no longer the dominant saver that it was before 1979, and faced a mounting budget deficit, it put pressure on state banks to finance such fixed investments using policy loans. In order to finance its extension of huge policy loans, the PBC has to collect amounts of money which are impressively large by international standards: almost 5 per cent of GDP.

Jin (1994) gave another explanation, which pointed out that the credit quotas of the banking system were largely used up for non-priority investments, and thus the government was obliged to permit further expansion of credit to target priority investments. Moreover, local governments had a bias towards new investments, rather than the 'technical transformation' investments required to renovate, upgrade, and better use existing capacity. Jin also indicated that tensions between central and local governments were the cause of credit expansion. The central government was concerned with aggregate credit expansion and local governments were competing to expand their individual industrial bases. Incompatibilities inherent in this situation are fuelled by the relatively unusual features of China's fiscal federalism, where the centre is a net recipient of resources from the provinces. An obvious question which follows is, what was the role of the banking system in this process? Leroy Jin (1994) explains that local branches of the central bank were largely subordinate to local governments, and were obliged to comply with their pressure to expand credit. Thus the behaviour and interests of the head office of the central bank could differ from its branch offices, and the appointment and dismissal of branch PBC directors needed local Communist Party Committee approval, at least until 1990.

Jinglian Wu (1995) analysed industry financing in order to give an explanation of the credit expansion. In 1979 decentralization changed the old scheme within which the central fiscal authority 'took in all the profits and paid out accounts' to the new system that local government and the central government will share the tax paid by enterprises. It had a deep impact on economic development thereafter. From the provincial and city governments down to the village and rural governments, all competed to set up factories and shops, duplicating distribution, without thinking about their comparative advantages and the optimal economic scale for the projects. These hurriedly established small firms competed for raw materials. Then the local governments carried out a protectionist policy for their own enterprises. They monopolized extremely scarce raw materials and energy, put up obstacles to prevent competing products from entering their own markets, and reduced and waived taxes for their own enterprises, giving them low interest loans and other preferential treatment. This system caused the local government to interfere in the professional activities of the banks at various levels. They did their utmost to use bank loans to support their efforts in realizing the economic goals of the region.

Each quarter, the branches of the PBC are allocated credit quotas by the headquarters, which they could use to provide advances to specialized banks. The various branches of the PBC and specialized banks are all under the leadership of local governments. Under their pressure, the branches of the PBC are likely to permit local banks to extend credit beyond the planned ceilings. In this context, the only investments local governments are willing to undertake are those within the confines of their jurisdictions, mainly in the shape of small-scale, profitable processing enterprises and even high-risk high-return investment such as real estate. In China, how much of the loans local enterprises will repay annually is in fact arranged by the local financial authorities. In other words, how much of the loans the banks can retrieve depends upon the decision of the local governments. In addition, the main allocation mechanism is through administration and not through the market, and government intervenes in all aspects of social activities. Despite efforts over recent years to strengthen the independence of the banks, the employees at each level of the bank system are appointed by the head office and its higher-level branches, so as to construct a vertical hierarchy within the banking system. However, the Party and Youth League affiliations of these employees still rest with the local region. The employees of the various financial institutions are subject to arrangements by local government for the supply of their medical care, housing and transportation. And the education and employment of the employee's children all depend upon local governments. This means that the interest of banks at different levels is closely linked to the interests of the local governments. The banks are therefore willing to do their best to serve the interests of the local governments, and there emerged a so-called 'regionalization' tendency in the banks' business activities (Wu, 1995). Every PBC branch has the tendency to give relending quotas only to those banks which make loans towards the enterprises under the same local government, and prevent money from flowing out, thus completely restricting the mobility of funds. The central bank cannot possibly control money supply through a unified financial market. Instead, it divides the monetary target among the local administrative areas and made local banks responsible for controlling money supply. According to Jinglian Wu (1995), in a situation where the aim of the monetary policy of the central bank is implemented through the dispersed control by the various regions, it is inevitable that they will compete to put money into circulation, creating the serious consequences of loss of control over the general volume of money and inflation.

2.6 Effects of the commercial banking reform

The commercial banks, which channel funds from depositors to the industrial enterprises, largely supported the industrial reform by introducing the modern financial intermediary. The commercial banks take advantage of standardization in their banking operations and develop professional financial service standards according to the concepts and practices of the modern financial intermediary. In the pre-reform capital markets in China, long-term investment was financed by the state budget through the PBC. The fund is directly allocated by the credit plan. The repayment was largely ignored. The good projects could not get funds and the 'bad' ones could not be punished because the state investment was not expected to be repaid anyway. Now the commercial banks have been spun off from the PBC. They managed the funds from many investors. By bundling many investors' business together, they can increase the size of transactions so that the cost per dollar investment decreases. The commercial banks screen and provide loans to high quality projects in industry. The industries, in the meantime, provide interest returns to the commercial banks. This dynamic cycle of mutual benefit contributes to the extraordinary success of the PRC's southern regions as a new vision of a market-dominated system shared by the

Communist Party. In that region, the government's contributions are only limited to the indirect macroeconomic controls.

According to Jefferson and Rawski (1994), regulations on 'Transforming the Management Mechanisms of State-owned Industrial Enterprises' reflect this new attitude, formalizing the autonomy of SOEs and their responsibility for the financial consequences of independent business decisions and of market-driven economic change. The text allows enterprises to reject or refuse official instructions, including mandatory plan directives, which still exist, but are limited to a narrowly defined boundary.

The reform of the profit-oriented commercial banking system, together with the rapid decline of price controls has pushed the industries to accept commercial lending standards. The success in decreasing the accumulation of the 'bad' loans could open the door to liberalization and diversification of domestic capital markets, which would in turn provide new opportunities as well as the financial discipline for Chinese enterprises. According to Jefferson and Rawski (1994), 'at the very least, the most recent reforms will have the desirable effect of consolidating industrial subsidies channeled through the banking system and making them more transparent than in the past'.

After these reforms, PBC lending to the commercial banks increased dramatically, as these banks began to take over the function of providing commercial credit from the monobank.

Figure 2.2 shows the annual level of lending by the PBC to the commercial banks and directly to industrial enterprises. The PBC conducted commercial banking business before 1981. The PBC granted

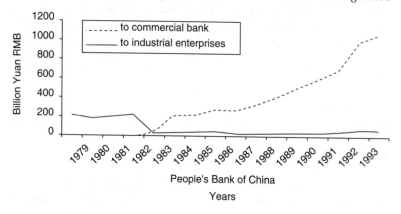

Figure 2.2 Annual lending by the PBC to commercial banks and industrial enterprises
Source: People's Bank of China, *ACFB*, 1994.

loans amounting to an average of 210 billion Yuan RMB annually to industrial enterprises, especially to SOEs, before 1981. Figure 2.2 also shows that the amount dropped to 30–73 billion Yuan RMB after 1983, when commercial banking business was transferred to the four specialized banks. The PBC has not conducted commercial banking business since 1983.

From Figure 2.2 we can also see that the central bank function of the PBC has been reinforced. Instead of credit planning, the PBC gives loans to the commercial banks at interest, called the discount rate. Thus discount loans increased dramatically from none in 1981 to 1000 billion in 1993. From 1979 to 1981, the financial market was the PBC monopoly, hence the PBC's loans to commercial banks were zero. Notice how the level of lending by the monobank to the commercial banks increases dramatically, whereas the level of monobank lending directly to industrial enterprises drops off after 1984.

The PBC (the monobank) has begun to act more like a central bank, making loans to commercial banks, at interest (the discount rate), and the commercial banks are beginning to make commercial loans on their own, as opposed to the previous system of government-directed lending and investment. The result was that commercial bank-directed lending to industrial enterprises for capital investment increased as a share of their total lending (including state-directed lending) from a very tiny proportion of total bank capital investment in 1979 to about 80 per cent of total bank capital investment by 1985 (World Bank, 1988), dramatically improving the efficiency of bank lending in China. Moreover, since the PBC got out of the business of making direct commercial loans, it has freed itself to act as a true central bank, focusing on the analysis of macroeconomic conditions and conducting monetary policy, thereby strengthening its control over the financial markets and maintaining monetary stability.

2.7 Summary

After the 1978–92 reforms, the commercial banking system was established. This not only built the base for sound financial intermediaries, but also relieved the central bank so that it could focus on the conduct of monetary policy.

Although a good beginning, there were still some major flaws in the new system. Since the previous banking system left 'bad' loans in the banking portfolios, non-performing loans were 50 per cent in some banks' balance sheets in the early 1980s. Some banks would have gone bankrupt if measured by the American commercial banking stand-ard. The high percentage of default loans made some banks' net worth negative.

In addition, deposits were administratively transferred by the regional head offices of the PBC from local branches with negative 'excess gaps' (loans net of deposits above the state-approved gap) to local branches with positive 'excess gaps'. This provided a disincentive to local branch bankers who were managing their loan portfolios efficiently.

However, if viewed from a wider perspective, the structure change of the Chinese banking system improved loan management and promoted Chinese economic development. This is what the Chinese banking reforms were designed for. It reflected the Chinese reformers' judge-ments: 'Men's judgements are a parcel of their fortunes' (Shakespeare, *Antony and Cleopatra*, III. xiii. 31).

3
Banking Reforms in 1993–7: Controlling Interest Rates

'The strawberry grows underneath the nettle.'

William Shakespeare, *Henry V*, I. i. 60

3.1 Introduction

Although the monetary policy apparatus described in the last chapter was in place by the mid-1980s, and the interest rate reform was discussed throughout that decade, the authorities of the People's Bank of China did not exercise its role as central banker, formulating and implementing monetary policy, until the summer of 1993 when inflation hit the Chinese economy.

The cause of the inflation can be traced back forty years. The Chinese government had concentrated on the manufacturing industry from 1953 to 1978. Under the centrally planned system, government controlled the price index factors such as exchange rate, salary level and interest rates in order to emphasize the manufacturing industry and build the 'high accumulation, heavy investment, high growth' development framework. The price system was frozen in this period and did not mirror the macroeconomic trend. The macroeconomic situation keeps a dynamic balance between the accumulation and the tendency to inflation. Between 1953 and 1978, the inflation pressure was low. The nominal GDP growth is not related to inflation growth. There was almost no inflation because of the mandatory pricing system.

The price reform

Before 1978, in the centrally planned economy, all the price levels, in both wholesale and retail sectors, were set by the government and had not changed for twenty years. The manipulated prices could not fit the new situation created by the 1978 reforms.

Price reform of the primary products such as grain, cotton, oil and coal was planned to take about twenty years from 1979, contributing to structural price increases of 3–5 percentage points annually. In the PRC, the reforms of the 1980s set the fixed low interest rates for loans made by state-owned and collective enterprises.

This round of reform of the pricing system caused inflation. In 1988 the consumer price index (CPI) inflated 18.53 per cent. The trend continued in 1989 with 17.78 per cent (Table 3.1).

To protect depositors from inflation, an interest rate subsidy scheme linked to the retail price index for the three or more years of certified deposit (CD) account was established on 1 September 1988. But it still could not match the high inflation rate of 18.53 per cent in 1988. People almost all over the country rushed into banks to withdraw savings deposits in a panic in 1988 and 1989.

Inflation in 1993

Deng Xiao-ping's tour to Shenzhen city in the early spring of 1992 started another wave of investment and development. During the tour, he suggested catching the international opportunity of development by increasing the reforming pace in China. When Premier Li Peng delivered the annual economic speech in the First Plenary Session of the Eighth National People's Congress on 15 March 1993, he emphasized the task in the next five years: to revise the GDP growth target to 8–9 per cent from the original 6 per cent. The purpose of this was to achieve the target that GDP in 2000 should be 400 per cent of that in 1980 (Yang, 1996). But at the time of his speech, he was not aware of the already growing inflation. The Chinese economy was on the way to overheating.

The administrative stimulation created an investment fever in 1992–3. Business demand for credit soared. From the second quarter of 1992 to the second quarter of 1993, huge sums were invested in the real estate market in the coastal areas. The financial institutions treated the inter-bank lending market as the easy and low-cost place to raise funds. Because of lack of central bank supervision (the legislation for the central bank itself did not appear until 1995), some of them even borrowed heavily from the inter-bank lending market to invest in long-term risky projects such as real estate in order to get high profits. The commercial banks and local governments circumvented the central bank's rules and regulations regarding acquiring deposits and making loans to industrial enterprises for new investment projects, including

Table 3.1 The Consumer price index (CPI) in the PRC from 1978 to 1997

	1978	1979	1980	1981	1982	1983	1984	1985	1986	1987	1988	1989	1990	1991	1992	1993	1994	1995	1996	1997
CPI	100	102.00	108.10	110.70	112.80	114.50	117.70	128.10	135.80	145.70	172.70	203.10	207.70	213.70	225.20	254.90	310.2	356.1	377.8	380.8
Inflation (%)	–	2.00	5.98	2.41	1.90	1.51	2.79	8.84	6.01	7.29	18.53	17.78	2.11	2.89	5.38	13.19	21.69	14.80	6.09	0.79

Source: China Statistics Yearbook 1998, for CPI data, taking 1978 data as 100.

real estate. The commercial banks also invested in risky stocks, usually at a loss.

In this situation, the central bank should have been aware of the situation and adjusted its monetary policy. According to the monetarists' view, the PBC should control potential inflation by affecting the high-powered money – net monetary liabilities of government held by the public, also called monetary base. According to the famous economist William Poole at the Federal Reserve Bank of St Louis, USA (1970), the PBC has another monetary policy tool to choose, the interest rate! But the PBC did not use either of them at the beginning.

Without the guidance of central banking monetary policy, Chinese bankers routinely underestimated the default risk on loans, and overestimated investment returns on new projects, especially real estate projects in early 1993. The banks also routinely exceeded their state-mandated 'gaps' and raised interest rates on deposits and loans to excessively high levels (sometimes exceeding 20 per cent on deposits and loans). The situation was similar to the excessive interest-rate competition among US banks in the 1920s, which precipitated the need for Regulation Q (the interest-rate ceiling provision included in the Glass-Steagall Act of 1933). With nothing to stop them in China, financial institutions chased profits by hiking the interest rate higher and higher.

According to the Chinese Statistical Bureau, in the first half of 1993 the growth rate of industry, fixed capital investment and GDP was 25 per cent, 61 per cent and 14 per cent, respectively. In the first half of the year, the total number of new projects increased by 15 per cent. Many new projects were to invest in the risky real estate business. Total investment was 125.7 billion Yuan RMB, double the amount in the same period the previous year.

By the summer of 1993 (end of the second quarter) a crisis situation emerged (Box 3.1). The budget deficit kept rising and the deposits in the commercial banks were insufficient to cover the development needs. Bank loans defaulted in record numbers. The total national value of savings deposits in the banking system dropped by 29 per cent (*China Statistics Yearbook*, 1997). Bank vault cash dropped to 4 per cent from its usual level of 10–20 per cent, and to less than 2 per cent for some banks. To make matters worse, there was a supply shortage of steel, electricity and transportation. The economy began to overheat. Currency (cash money) in circulation rose by 54.9 billion Yuan to a record of 552.8 billion Yuan (People's Bank of China, *Almanac of China's Finance and Banking*, 1998), and the inflation rate was rising at an annual rate of more than 13.19 per cent in 1993 and 21.69 per cent in 1994 (Table 3.1).

Box 3.1 Three types of financial disorders in the 1993 inflation crisis in the PRC

1. Fund collection disorders: funds were collected by the authorities, the collective organizations, individuals, provinces, cities and counties. Collected funds in the first quarter of 1993 amounted to 50 billion Yuan, dramatically removing deposits from banks. Some of the money was invested into real estate or smuggling.
2. Inter-bank lending disorders: some banks lent money to non-bank institutions for profit-making purposes because rates could be charged in contravention of the regulations. This also increased the supply of money.
3. Banking disorders: in order to escape the central bank's supervision, some banks set up economic entities for profit-making investment, calling this 'a combination of banking and trading with varied business'. The State Council published a series of documents to stop these, but the power to do so by administrative methods was limited as it required further steps to reform the banking system.

Source: *People's Daily* (25 July 1993), translated by Yang (1996).

The RMB exchange rate in un-official markets had declined sharply from 7.4 Yuan per US dollar in January 1993 to 11 Yuan per US dollars in June 1993.

It was time for the PBC to control inflation. But how should the PBC react? This question was presented to Chinese central bankers who had only nine years of experience since the Chinese central bank was officially established in 1984.

3.2 Theories of controlling inflation

Regarding the origin of inflation, traditional theories include demand-driven inflation, cost-driven inflation and structural inflation. A detailed discussion will be far beyond this book's range. Here we only introduce the theories related to the question 'how should the government act to control inflation?'

There are three major opinions regarding the government's role in the control of inflation. One opinion is derived from the monetarists' view that price inflation is caused by money supply, thus (of course) it can be cured by money supply contraction. Another is the structural inflation theory. It argues that the inflation is built into the social structure. The reform should allow a certain level of inflation. As long as there is a balance between inflation and economic development, some inflation should be allowed and cannot be avoided. The third opinion is that government should not intervene in the economy, and that government's intervention will make things worse. The only thing government can do is to liberalize financial markets and let the free market determine how to allocate credit. This opinion is related to the 'shock treatment', which was prevalent in Russia and Eastern Europe in the early 1990s.

The monetarists' view, as put forward by Milton Friedman, states that inflation is a monetary phenomenon in any circumstances. Their assumption is the extremely free market system. In the free market, the concept that economic stability correlates to price stability has the same meaning as the concept that the actual supply equals the potential supply. Thus, price stability is the only condition for the rapid growth of the economy. According to Perkins (1994), in a market system, inflation is controlled by government actions that determine the amount of high-powered money. In turn, the amount of high-powered money determines the supply of money, including deposits of the banking system, that is the main source of supply of loans to business. Business demand for credit determines how many loans are actually made.

The monetarists' view has great success in explaining the inflation pathway from money supply to price inflation, but it cannot trace the pathway backward by saying that the microeconomic result of repressing inflation is only a monetary phenomenon. In practice, if the policymaker prematurely chases the target of price stability by only using the money supply as the monetary policy tool, the economic growth target will probably not be achieved. Instead, it will eventually cause deflation and no growth of GDP.

Some studies (Xiao-xi Li, 1991) on the Chinese data confirm the above analysis. They use the structural inflation model to analyse different price adjustment procedures in the manufacturing, service, agriculture and other sectors in China. Price adjustments by the Chinese government in the economic reforms produced the potential for inflation. If the price elasticity is low and the base price cannot drop, price adjustments in different economic sectors will inevitably lead to inflation. Thus government policies can do little to control inflation.

Zheng (1999) raised three sequential questions against the structural inflation theories in assessing the effectiveness of the government intervention to fight inflation.

1. Is central government able to control inflation? At what level?
   The experience of fighting inflation in China showed that the loosening or tightening of macroeconomic policies has an important influence on the initiation, level and termination of inflation. So the answer to question 1 is 'yes'.
2. Is inflation correlated to economic growth?
3. If the answer to question 2 is 'no', the government should focus on economic growth goals, if inflation does not increase to an unacceptable level. If the answer to question 2 is 'yes', how shall the government choose the proper policies to balance the economic growth target and the inflation control target?

According to Zheng (1999), the structural inflation theory is not constant in theoretical orientation and policy recommendation. In theory, the structural inflation supporters think that the reason for inflation is the political and economic structure. Government behaviour is decided by the structure, and all macroeconomic policy choices depend on the structure. Thus, the existing inflation will develop according to its own rules without being affected by the policy. However, in policy suggestions, the supporters criticized government policy defects and tried to give some policy advice, thereby conceding that policies do have effects on inflation. This inconsistency showed that policies do have influence on inflation.

The supporters of the extreme anti-inflation theory do not admit the correlation and balance transfer between inflation and economic growth and give the answer 'no' to question 2. They avoid question 3 and think that government should not fight inflation unless inflation is severe. They support their ideas by showing econometric analysis of postwar development. Zheng (1999) challenged them by indicating that the developing countries as a group deviated from the average trend of the econometric data. In addition, only analysing the Asian 'tigers' left other Asian developing countries out of the econometric analysis and decreased the sample size.

McKinnon (1973) and Shaw (1973) showed that government intervention causes low savings, credit rationing and low investment. The effects are through three channels: firstly, through the marginal productivity of capital. When the interest rate is lower than the equilibrium rate of interest, high-quality projects are not undertaken. Secondly, there is the financial repression effect on the return to savings allocated to investment. Thirdly, through its effect on the return to savings, it also affects the equilibrium level of savings and investment.

Thus, the policy will rely on removal of interest rate ceilings, reduction of reserve requirements and abolition of directed credit programmes: in short, to liberalize the financial markets and let the free market determine the allocation of credit. As the interest rate adjusts to its equilibrium level, low-yielding investment projects would be eliminated. Then the overall efficiency of investment would be enhanced. Also, as the interest rate increases, savings and the total real supply of credit increases, inducing a higher volume of investment. Economic development would, therefore, be stimulated not only through increased investment but also due to an increase in the average productivity of capital. Moreover, the effects of lower reserve requirements reinforce the effects of higher savings on the supply of bank lending, while the abolition of directed credit programmes would lead to an even more efficient allocation of credit, thereby further stimulating the average productivity of capital (Arestis and Demetriades, 1999).

The above theories have to be related to the Chinese situation in order to solve the problem of inflation in the PRC. Interest rates were manually set by the Chinese government at a level lower than that of equilibrium. High interest rates in 1993 resulted in projects with high qualities being unlikely to be undertaken according to the theory of adverse selection. People had a feeling of shrinking wealth when comparing inflation rates with bank savings rates, and were likely to withdraw money from banks. It might even induce a banking crisis.

3.3 Using interest rates to control inflation

Facing the inflation, the government and the authorities of the PBC decided to act. The 1993 banking reforms followed. Four policies were used: administrative control, banking system reforms, the interest rate tool, and legal regulation.

The administrative controls included the announcement of government regulatory rules, credit planning controls, business restrictions by local governments and foreign exchange controls. All those included administrative procedures issued by the State Planning Commission as the famous 'the Sixteen Regulations in 1993' (this is related to fiscal policies and beyond the scope of this book) and monetary policy procedures issued by PBC as quoted in Box 3.2.

Box 3.2 Ten regulations to prevent the increase of interest rates, June 1993

1. Financial institutions must follow the PBC interest rates guideline;
2. PBC is the only organization in China allowed to set interest rates;
3. Commercial banks must not increase interest rates above the PBC ceiling;
4. Working capital loans shall float no more than 20 per cent higher/10 per cent lower than PBC rates;
5. Corporate bond rates should not be higher than the T-bill rates;
6. Borrowing between banks should not go beyond the PBC interest rates;
7. Firms without PBC licences should not undertake savings and loan business;
8. Financial institutions shall report interest rates to PBC periodically;
9. Those who do not obey the above regulations must pay a fine;
10. PBC branches shall supervise the rates of commercial banks and other financial institutions.

Source: People's Bank of China, *Almanac of China's Finance and Banking*, 1994.

PBC analysed the economic conditions periodically and adjusted the total amount of loans in order to meet the market demand by the state key investments. After July 1993, PBC Chairman Zhu Rongji hosted eight meetings of the central bankers to analyse the economic situation, loan distribution and money demand, and solved the problems according to different situations. He visited 15 provinces with other central bankers to investigate the local situations and solved some financial problems during these visits.

During the 1993 reform, the central bank for the first time took advantage of the control of interest rates as a monetary policy tool (Box 3.3).

Box 3.3 Facts of interest rate adjustment as a monetary policy tool, 1993–8 (Table 3.2)

- The PBC changed interest rates three times with a total arise of 342 basis points in 1993 for one-year loans to banks (from 7.2 to 10.62).
- In January and July of 1995, when the economy overheated, the central bank increased the interest rates twice (in January, it increased the rate from 10.62 per cent to 10.89 per cent (Table 3.2), and in July increased the rate to 11.16 per cent).
- Because the retail price index dropped in 1998, the PBC decreased the interest rate several times in 1998.

Source: China Statistics Yearbook, 1994–9.

PBC chairman Zhu Rongji told financial institution leaders in the MOF meeting, 5–7 July 1993, that they should follow three rules as shown in Box 3.4.

Box 3.4 Speech of the PBC chairman Zhu Rongji at the Ministry of Finance meeting, 5–7 July 1993

1. The immediate cessation and clearance of all irregular inter-bank lending, such loans to be retrieved by the banks within a specified date;
2. No financial institutions would be allowed to raise deposit and loan interest rates, nor launch a 'deposit taking battle' or take any commission from debtors;
3. The immediate cessation of crediting economic entities established by the financial institutions themselves – banks should separate themselves from the varied investment economic entities they had established.

Zhu Rongji made it clear that this period of macroeconomic adjustment and control did not represent a national financial retrenchment.

Source: Yang, 1996.

Table 3.2 Changes of benchmark interest rates* in the PRC by the PBC, 1991–2001

Date of Changing	21/8/90	21/4/91	1/4/93	15/5/93	11/7/93	1/1/95	1/7/95	1/5/96	23/8/96	23/10/97	25/3/98	1/7/98	7/12/98	10/6/99
Interest rate for reserves	6.84	6.12			9.18	9.18	9.18	8.82	8.28	7.56	5.22	3.51	3.24	2.07
Loans to Banks (1 year)	7.92	7.2	7.38	9.00	10.62	10.89	11.16	10.98	10.62	9.36	7.92	5.67	5.13	3.78
Loans to banks (20 days)	7.92	7.2	6.84	8.46	10.08	10.26	10.44	9.0	9.0	8.55	6.39	5.22	4.59	3.24
Certified deposit (CD) (1 year)	8.64	7.56		9.18	10.98				7.47	5.67	5.22	4.77	3.78	2.25
Flow capital Loans (1 year)	9.36	8.64		9.36	10.98	10.98	12.06		10.08	8.64	7.92	6.93	6.39	5.85

*The Chinese central bank uses one-year discount rate as their benchmark rate because 80 per cent of the loans to commercial banks are for at least one year. The commercial banks in the PRC have not started to use overnight discount loans to cover their reserve requirements as in the USA. Also banks can overlook reserve requirement policy because the central bank carries more of the loan quota to banks.
Source: China Statistics Yearbook, 1998–2001; *Interest Rates Brochure*, People's Bank of China, Wuhan Branch, 1999.

3.4 The separation of commercial banking from investment banking business

Introduction

In the wave of investment in 1992–3, some financial institutions treated the inter-bank lending market as an easy and low-cost place to raise funds. Because of lack of central bank's supervision (the legislation for the central bank itself did not appear until 1995), some of them even borrowed heavily from the inter-bank lending market to invest in real estate. Some commercial banks were also chasing high profits by investing in risky stocks.

As described earlier, without the legislation to separate commercial banking from the investment banking business, bankers routinely underestimated risks on the stock market and overestimated investment returns on securities. In 1993 Chinese commercial banks speculated stocks by moving savings deposit funds into the stock markets. By the summer of 1993, deposits in the commercial banks were insufficient to cover development needs. To solve these problems, Chinese central bankers learned from the US in separating commercial banking from investment banking business that is related to the securities markets.

Theories and policy implications

An important feature of the structure of the banking industry in the US history was the separation of the banking and security industry although this separation no longer exists. The Glass-Steagall Act of 1933 forced a separation between these industries. Glass-Steagall Act allowed commercial banks to sell new offerings of government securities but prohibited them from underwriting corporate securities or from engaging in brokerage activities. It also prohibited investment banks from engaging in commercial banking activities and thus had protected commercial banks from competition.

Commercial banks have an unfair advantage in competing against brokerage firms. In the US, deposits provide commercial banks with an artificially low cost of funds because they are insured by the FDIC. In China, the same thing is true because the deposits are insured by the PBC and the four commercial banks belong to the state. However, brokerage firms have higher costs on the funds they acquire, which are usually obtained through loans from the banks.

Commercial banks will have a potential conflict of interest if they engage in underwriting of securities. Banks that underwrite new issues of securities will sell them to trust funds that they manage when they cannot sell them to anyone else, and these trust funds often take big losses when the securities are sold later. This will make the total quality of the bank assets low and eventually could result in a bank failure.

The securities businesses, conducted by investment banks, are risky, and could face dramatic losses. If the commercial banks are allowed to undertake securities business, the deposit and the interest may not get paid in the circumstances of investment loss. Moral hazard and adverse selection problems (see Chapter 5.2) will also occur through commercial banks taking additional risks, if the commercial banks are allowed to undertake investment business.

After the US economy suffered huge losses in the Great Depression, partially due to commercial banks taking on investment-banking business, the US Congress passed the Glass-Steagall Act in 1933. It separated commercial banking from investment banking business. Commercial banks are forbidden to invest in stock markets. Additional regulations prohibited banks from selling insurance and engaging in other non-bank activities that were considered risky.

Separation of commercial banking from investment banking business

In June 1993 the PBC issued an announcement entitled 'Some Opinions Regarding the Current Economic Situation' (which was the Chinese equivalent of the provision for the separation of commercial banking from investment banking as in the Glass-Steagall Act of 1933). This announcement is translated in Boxes 3.5.

The independence of the central bank

As indicated by Gautier (Gautier, 1990), the banks in a market economy need a central bank. The financial chaos in America in the early twentieth century created the environment to form the Federal Reserve Bank in the US. China had the same situation while on the way to the market economy.

On 14 November 1993 the PBC obtained official permission from the Chinese Communist Party Central Committee to become totally independent in conducting the monetary policy. In a memorandum (see Box 3.6) the financial supervision function of the PBC was emphasized.

Another important development at the time was the appointment of Chinese Premier Zhu Rongji as Chairman of the People's Bank of China. On the positive side, this increased the power of the PBC, giving it the power to act decisively. On the negative side, it made

Box 3.5   Some opinions regarding the current economic situation, June 1993

Due to the high inflation in 1993, the PBC has decided to increase interest rates. The PBC will focus on enforcing financial supervision; separating state-owned commercial banks from their affiliated trust and investment firms; requiring all specialized banks to call back loans made outside the credit plan immediately; restricting inter-regional lending; sending out working groups to the provinces to check the implementation of these measures. Four policy measures are being implemented: clearing up and withdrawing loans granted without authorization; raising interest rates on deposits and loans; restraining irregular capital-raising activities and restoring order among investments in real estate and development areas.

Source: People's Bank of China, *ACFB: Almanac of China's Finance and Banking*, 1994.

Box 3.6   Memorandum of the Chinese Communist Party Central Committee, 14 November 1993

- As the central bank, the People's Bank of China shall conduct monetary policy independently.
- The People's Bank of China shall be under the leadership of the State Council.
- The People's Bank of China shall manage the money supply and stabilize the currency value, by changing from relying mainly on control over the credit quota to the reserve ratio control.
- The People's Bank of China shall supervise all other financial institutions.
- The People's Bank of China will not conduct business with non-financial institutions.
- The banking business and the securities business shall be separated.
- A committee shall be formed to conduct monetary policy.
- The commercial banks shall engage in the management of assets, liabilities and risks.

Box 3.6 (*continued*)

- According to the situation of money supply and demand, the central bank shall make timely adjustments of the benchmark rates.
- The interest rates of the deposits and loans in the commercial banks can be freely floated within a certain range given by the PBC.

Source: People's Bank of China, ACFB: *Almanac of China's Finance and Banking*, 1994.

---

the central bank even less independent than it was before, which could cause problems in the future.

According to Yang (1996):

> Budget deficits are financed most easily by central banks, but central banks have a responsibility to restrict the budget deficit in order to control inflation. There were 7 years out of 11 years after banking decentralization in China when Chinese government borrowing was larger than its deposits into the PBC. In some years inflation either accompanied or followed such overdrafts. This indicates that a government facing great pressures during transaction may need the help of a strong central bank on one hand. Increasing the independence of central banks may help to restrict budget borrowing and overdrawing from the banking system on the other hand.

Following the 1993 reforms, the PBC began to take a more active role in managing the monetary system. The bank began to change the discount rate, increasing it twice, in April and May and then again in July, in an effort to curb inflation. From April to May the discount rate was increased 180 basis points, from 7.2 per cent to 9 per cent, and in July the discount rate was increased another 162 basis points to 10.62 per cent (*China Statistics Yearbook*, 1997, also Table 3.2). At the same time, the bank increased its lending to state enterprises and to the agricultural sector. This was necessary to subsidize the rising costs of inflation in these sectors. These loans are called 'policy loans'.

Box 3.7 List of laws passed in 1993 to tackle financial disorder

- 9 August 1993: *The Regulation of Enterprise Debt Management,* which makes clear the process and qualifications of the enterprise debt issuance.
- 2 September 1993: *The Anti-Trust Law of the PRC,* which defines unfair competition and makes clear the supervision, investigation and legal implications of unfair competition.
- 6 September 1993: *The Law of Economic Contracts of the PRC,* which strengthens the management of economic contracts and makes clear the implications of any violation of the contracts.
- 19 September 1993: The Current Regulation of State Public Administrators.

Source: People's Daily, various issues, 1993.

In the control of interest rates in 1993, the PBC was supported by legislation from the People's Congress. Box 3.7 lists some of the legislation passed in 1993 in the battle against inflation and financial disorder.

3.5 Results of the 1993 reform

These policies did result in some improvement in the economy. Comparing the second half of 1993 with the first half, economic conditions marginally improved. In the second half of the year, 80 per cent of all new loans directed to industrial enterprises in 1993 were made (People's Bank of China, *China Monthly Statistics Summary,* 1993). In addition, in the second half of the year, savings deposits increased by 102.6 billion Yuan to 2151.88 billion Yuan, whereas in the first half of the year savings deposits dropped by 22.6 billion Yuan (*China Statistics Yearbook,* 1997). In 1994 net savings averaged 35.9 per cent of total savings (Table 3.3). The urban credit corporations contributed the biggest net savings proportion (48.2 per cent) and commercial banks contributed the biggest net savings amount (711.3 billion Yuan RMB). Compared with the panic withdrawal of deposits in some cities in the summer of 1993, the savings increase in 1994 showed the success of the 1993 interest rate operation by the PBC.

Most importantly, in the second half of the year, inflation grew at an annual rate of 17.6 per cent, down from over 23 per cent in the first half of the year (a slight improvement), but inflation continued to grow in

Table 3.3 1994 increase of savings (billion Yuan)

	Saving change	Loan change	Net	% change
Commercial banks	3048.8	2337.5	711.3	23.3
Trust	512.0	316.4	195.6	38.2
Rural credit corp.	1383.9	913.5	470.4	33.9
Urban credit corp.	989.7	512.6	477.1	48.2
Other banks	372.2	248.2	124.0	33.3
Total	11269.3	7216.6	4052.7	35.9

Source: *China Statistics Yearbook*, 1995.

1994 at a rate of 21.5 per cent (slightly worse than the inflation rate in 1993, which was 20.4 per cent for the year). So the monetary policy actions taken in 1993 did not immediately stabilize the economy. Inflation persisted for several years to come. Further action would be needed to stabilize the economy.

In addition, Table 3.4 shows the good outcome of the central bank control of interest rates. The 1993 increase of savings deposits was low (only 252 billion Yuan RMB more than that of 1992). After 1993 it had a net increase of 345 billion in 1994, 632 billion in 1995. Money supply in 1993 was 152.9 billion, increasing by 35.3 per cent which was lower than that of 1992. Thus the central bank intervention in 1993 effectively controlled the over-supply of currency. This was a real success. In China the interest rate has not played an important role as a monetary policy tool. Enterprises are still largely depending on the low interest rate directly allocated by the state-owned commercial banks. Even after the enterprise reform, this allocation of loans still exists. The only change is that the pre-reform credit rationing becomes 'loan-rationing' now. So enterprises are inelastic to the interest rate change.

Table 3.4 Bank savings statistics, 1991–6 (billion Yuan RMB)

Year	Savings deposits of urban & rural residents	In which: Time deposits	Savings deposits in urban area	In which: Time deposits	Farmer's savings deposits	In which: Time deposits
1991	924.16	769.15	692.49	580.86	231.67	188.29
1992	1175.80	946.16	889.07	718.66	286.73	227.50
1993	1520.35	1197.10	1162.73	912.58	357.62	284.52
1994	2151.88	1683.87	1670.30	1302.80	481.60	381.06
1995	2966.23	2377.82	2346.70	1876.50	619.56	501.32
1996	3852.08	3087.34	3085.00	2457.90	767.06	629.44

Source: *China Statistics Yearbook*, 1997.

3.6 The 1994–7 reforms: money supply as a monetary policy tool

Introduction

On and before 1994, China had strict foreign currency restrictions, which means that free foreign exchange in the market is forbidden. When enterprises needed foreign currency for foreign trade, they had to report to the Bank of China (before 1978, it was the PBC) how much foreign currency they needed. Then the BOC would investigate and approve the application and allocate an approved amount of foreign currency to the enterprise, at a government-defined exchange rate. This rate did not reflect the supply and demand relationship in the foreign exchange market. For example, the BOC gave US dollars to the enterprises at the rate of one dollar equal to 4–5 Yuan RMB in 1990. But in the black market the rate was 7–8.

This favourable exchange rate can be treated as a subsidy to the enterprises. They used cheap money to buy foreign machines and materials as inputs to production. In the meantime the products were sold at the much higher market equilibrium prices. In addition, even in the domestic market, the government also manually set the low price for the input materials for enterprises. Both of the above procedures created the so-called 'dual price' system.

This is not the economic equilibrium condition. According to Perkins (1994), there are five steps to make a market work well: (1) achieve macro stability; (2) make inputs and outputs available for purchase and sales on the market, rather than allocated administratively through a state bureaucracy; (3) free up prices to reflect relative scarcities in the economy; (4) remove barriers to market entry so that competition between firms in different localities becomes possible; (5) change key elements of the institutional framework so that decision-makers in the production unit have an incentive to maximize profits by cutting their costs or raising sales. In China, the industry reform that began in 1984 was trying to follow some of those steps to make the market work well. After achieving macroeconomic stability, China tried to break state bureaucracy in the allocation of inputs and outputs.

As economic reform deepened, the region where the foreign companies could set up their own or joint venture firms expanded from the south-east coast in 1979 to the whole country in 1990s. More and more foreign companies came to China to do business directly with local enterprises and companies in other sectors. The demand for foreign currency rose quickly. The BOC could no longer restrict foreign exchange by subsidizing enterprises at a lower exchange rate. Otherwise the BOC would keep losing money. The exchange rate must reflect the real economic equilibrium level.

In 1994 the PRC reformed the foreign exchange system. The exchange rate is allowed to float in a certain range. Foreign currency has no more restrictions. Domestic and foreign enterprises and companies are free to use foreign currency for daily operations. Because of the international trade surplus, China has to trade in foreign currencies in the foreign exchange market in order to keep the RMB exchange rate stable. The money supply is executed in the foreign exchange market through open market operations. The BOC buys foreign currencies and sells RMB in the foreign exchange market. At the same time, the PBC counteracts the operation by recalling discount loans in the domestic money market to balance it. Starting from 1995, monetary policy began to consider the international trade balance and the foreign currency assets and liabilities in the banks. The exchange rate became the target and the money supply became the major monetary policy tool.

Theories and policy implication

In all market transactions in the economy, money in the form of currency or cheques is a medium of exchange, unit of account and store of value. The Federal Reserve Bank of the US defines the money supply as follows.

The narrowest definition of money is M1, which corresponds to the definition proposed by the theoretical approach and includes currency, chequing account deposits, and traveller's cheques. M2 monetary aggregate adds to M1 the money market deposit accounts, money market mutual fund shares, small-denomination time deposits, savings deposits, overnight repurchase agreements and overnight Eurodollars. The M3 monetary aggregate adds to M2 somewhat less liquid assets such as large-denomination time deposits, term repurchase agreements, term Eurodollars and institutional money market mutual fund shares. The final measure, L, which is really not a measure of money at all but rather a measure of highly liquid assets, adds to M3 several types of securities that are essentially highly liquid bonds, such as short-term treasury securities, commercial paper, savings bonds and banker's acceptances.

The money supply as the monetary policy tool is used in open market operations. Taking the US as an example, the open market operation decision is made by the Federal Open Market Committee (FOMC). The FOMC has 12 members consisting of the seven governors of the Federal Reserve System and the presidents of five of the district banks.

When the FOMC wants to increase the money supply, it purchases US government securities in the open market. It pays for these securities by creating new bank reserves, and these additional reserves lead to a multiple expansion of the money supply. An open market purchase of bonds by the central bank not only raises the money supply but also drives up bond prices and pushes interest rates down. Conversely, an open market sale of bonds, which decreases the money supply, lowers bond prices and raises interest rates.

The central bank also sets the minimum required reserve ratio and controls lending to banks to control the money supply.

The central banking system in the US was established in 1914. It has the following components: Federal Reserve Banks, the Board of Governors of the Federal Reserve System, the Federal Open Market Committee, the Federal Advisory Council and about 4000 member commercial banks. Most of the power resides in the seven-member Board of Governors of the Federal Reserve System and especially in its Chairman, Alan Greenspan, an economist. Members of the board are appointed by the President of the United States for a 14-year term. They are independent of the rest of the government and have responsibility for determining the national monetary policy. The power of appointment gives the President considerable long-run influence over the Federal Reserve policy.

The US Federal Reserve System provides a model for the Chinese central bank to learn from.

1995 reform: legislation for the Chinese central bank

To pave the way for monetary policy reform, it was necessary to reorganize the Chinese central bank in such a way as to separate the monetary-policy-making apparatus of the bank from the fiscal-policy-apparatus of the central government. That is, the central bank had to be made more independent from the government to avoid conflicts of interest in controlling the monetary system. To accomplish this, it was necessary to spin off the policy loan management arm of the central bank into a separate entity outside the bank (the newly created policy banks). The central bank would then be free from political interference. This was accomplished in a PBC branch chiefs' meeting announcement on 31 January 1995, after a routine meeting of the Board with the branch chiefs. Transferring the responsibility for making so-called 'policy loans' from the central bank to the newly created policy banks partially insulated the bank from government policy interference by isolating it from the process of subsidizing the government-controlled sectors of the economy. The text of the 31 January announcement is translated in Box 3.8.

Box 3.8   Memo stating the decisions taken at the People's Bank of China branch chiefs meeting on 31 January 1995

- The district branches shall calculate the assets and liabilities of the policy loan operations of the People's Bank of China from the balance sheets of the commercial banks in their district.
- The district branches shall prepare to separate policy loan operations from the balance sheets of the commercial banks [on behalf of the central bank] and transfer these operations to the newly created policy banks.

Table 3.5 is the balance sheet of Chinese Agriculture Development Bank (ADB). On the assets side, short-term assets increased steadily at an average annual growth rate of 15–22 per cent. The short-term policy loans to agriculture are a big proportion of the total short-term assets, having a range from 80 per cent to 89 per cent. Long-term policy loans to the agriculture sector are almost the total long-term assets excluding bank capital. The ADB indeed took over the PBC's previous job on policy loans to agriculture so that the PBC could be free from political interference to focus on the central banking business. Of course, it is worth pointing out that the 'bad' loans are almost 2 per cent of the long-term loans in the ADB. Borrowing from the central bank is the major source of funds.

Table 3.6 is the balance sheet of the State Development Bank (SDB). On the assets side, the long-term policy loans to state key development projects were 266.17 billion Yuan RMB in 1996, which was 95 per cent of its total assets. It shows the focus of the SDB. In 1997 this number was 96 per cent. The 'bad' loans in SDB were very small. On the liability side, the funds mainly came from issuing bonds.

Table 3.7 is the balance sheet of Chinese Import-Export Bank. On the assets side, policy loans mainly go to support the import export projects. On the liability side, the fund mainly came from issuing bonds.

The central bank was now free to concentrate on the conduct of monetary policy. As discussed in section 3.3, the authorities of the PBC issued two announcements in June, 1993 ('Ten Regulations Preventing the Increase of Interest Rates' (Box 3.2) and 'Some Opinions Regarding the Current Economic Situation' (Box 3.5)), which implemented phase one of its monetary policy reforms. Those announcements mandated that only the central bank was allowed to set interest

Table 3.5 Policy bank: Chinese Agriculture Development Bank (billion Yuan RMB)

Asset	1995	1996	1997	Liability	1995	1996	1997
1. Short-term assets	403.794	494.425	571.161	1. Short-term	530.565	688.496	883.550
Cash	0.004	0.154	0.309	Saving	27.661	38.515	45.487
Saving in central bank	22.243	33.714	26.223	Borrow from central bank	445.011	609.692	816.779
Reserve	1.803	2.128	3.449	Between banks	27.674	11.194	0.798
Between banks	25.264	11.603	2.859	Other	30.219	29.095	20.486
Short-term loan	326.951	404.218	508.863	2. Long-term	0.009	10.764	27.570
Other	27.529	42.608	29.458	Issue bonds	0	10.750	27.527
2. Long-term asset	138.686	217.985	352.062	Other	0.009	0.014	0.043
Loan	141.807	220.582	354.945	3. Other	11.939	13.189	12.180
('Bad' loan)	3.563	4.686	6.361				
Capital	0.169	0.473	0.747				
Other	0.273	1.616	2.731				
3. Other	0.033	0.039	0.077				

Source: People's Bank of China, ACFB: Almanac of China's Finance and Banking (1998).

Table 3.6 Policy bank: State Development Bank (billion Yuan RMB)

Asset	1996	1997	Liability	1996	1997
Cash	0.02262	0.05405	Short-term saving	0.84821	1.29291
Saving in central bank	0.10615	1.08697	Between banks	0.08298	
Between banks	5.42740	4.34565	Bill	23.32387	21.25506
Short-term between banks	0.09958	0.29807	Other bill	0.09666	1.41042
Short-term from financial firms	0.04979	0.00828	Social welfare	−0.00178	−0.00171
Short-term loan	0.75016	0.44544	Tax	1.87150	1.18874
Loan payment	0.46435	0.15766	Issue bonds	218.00649	305.34371
('Bad' loan)	0.00749	0.00143	Long-term borrowing	1.72047	4.95169
Other	2.59274	1.56615	Other	2.39661	0.00291
Short-term investment	0.65074	0.40549	Other liability	31.93528	45.70454
Long-term loan	266.1747	365.1822			
('Bad' loan)	1.69388	2.66925			
Long-term investment	4.15078				
Capital	0.03437	0.03357			
On-going project	0.60535	0.73482			
Other	1.60098	0.00846			
TOTAL	280.2803	381.14827		280.2803	381.14827

Source: People's Bank of China, ACFB: Almanac of China's Finance and Banking (1998).

Table 3.7 Policy bank: Chinese Import–Export Bank (billion Yuan)

Asset	1995	1996	1997	Liability	1995	1996	1997
Between banks	2.63463	5.14848	3.84681	Between banks	0.23290	1.10063	0.94013
Short- & long-term loan	7.15813	14.51421	24.80952	Debt	0.09743	0.15148	0.18524
('Bad' loan)	0.02000	0.08554	0.15964	Guarantee payment	0.02385	0.08991	0.00845
Loan payment	0.26314	1.56182	1.95870	Other bill	0.59653	1.10576	1.25523
('Bad' loan)	0.00008	0.00028	0.00062	Issue bonds	7.40000	16.03601	24.47389
Capital	0.01934	0.04058	0.05140	Reserve	0.01484	0.05921	0.11658
(Capital depreciation)	0.00276	0.00656	0.01168	Treasury dept	0.50000	0.50000	0.84853
On-going project	0.13686	0.19830	0.46279	Other	1.38044	2.51826	3.48927
Long-term investment		0.0005	0.01043				
Other	0.01105	0.00500	0.00573				
TOTAL	10.24599	21.56127	31.31732		10.24599	21.56127	31.31732

Source: People's Bank of China, *ACFB: Almanac of China's Finance and Banking* (1998).

rates. As interest-rate policy was the only policy tool at the time, this meant that the PBC was formally assuming its policy-making role. But the bank's interest-rate monetary policy regime will have more effect in controlling inflation and stabilizing the economy. It was now time to expand the central bank's menu of policy tools and broaden its mandate to control the money supply.

New legislation was introduced on 18 March 1995, which gave the PBC sweeping powers to supervise and regulate the banking system, and to conduct monetary policy to stabilize and expand the economy. This legislation was designed to give the central bank the tools necessary to manage the banking system and regulate the monetary economy in accordance with accepted modern central banking principles used in Western capitalist countries. In particular, Section 4 of the 18 March legislation established the central bank use of: reserve ratio requirements in Article 1; discount loans to commercial banks, including the setting of the discount rate in Articles 2 and 4; and the conduct of some form of open market purchase and sale of government securities to control the money supply in Article 5. The 18 March legislation is translated in Box 3.9.

Box 3.9   Act of the People's Bank of China: legislation passed by the People's Congress, 18 March 1995

Chapter 1   General

1. The purpose of this banking law is to define the status and responsibility of the People's Bank of China. To guarantee that state monetary policy be formed and implemented correctly. To set up and improve the system of central bank macro-regulation. To supervise financial markets.
2. The People's Bank of China is the central bank of China. It sets monetary policy and supervises financial markets.
3. The goal of monetary policy is to stabilize the value of the currency and help to expand the economy.
4. Responsibilities of the People's Bank of China
    (i) Setting monetary policy
    (ii) Issuing and managing the currency: RMB
    (iii) According to law, to license and supervise financial institutions
    (iv) Supervising financial markets

Box 3.9 (*continued*)

   (v) Setting regulation and orders of financial supervision
  (vi) Holding and managing the foreign currency reserves and gold reserves
 (vii) Managing the state treasury
(viii) Maintaining the operation of the payments and clearing system
  (ix) Taking responsibility for financial statistics investigation, analysis and forecast
   (x) As the state's central bank, to participate in international financial transactions
  (xi) Other responsibilities set by the State Council.

5. The People's Bank of China sets and operates annual currency supply, interest rates, exchange rates, and other decisions made by the State Council.
6. The People's Bank of China annually reports to the People's Congress Standing Committee.
7. Under the leadership of the State Council People's Bank of China conducts monetary policy independently without interference from any local governments, social organizations, or any person.
8. The People's Bank of China's assets belong to the state.

Chapter 2 Organization

9. The People's Bank of China has one chairman and several vice-chairmen who are decided by the People's Congress and nominated by the premier.
10. The chairman takes full responsibility for the operations of the People's Bank of China. The vice-chairmen act as aides to the chairman.
11. The People's Bank of China has the Monetary Policy Committee.
12. The People's Bank of China sets up branches in local cities wherever needed.
13. The chairman and all the employees of the People's Bank of China must obey the state laws, perform their duties, must not engage in unlawful business, and must not take any outside position in any other financial institution, industrial enterprise or foundation.
14. All employees of the People's Bank of China should not release national secrets.

Box 3.9 *(Continued)*

Chapter 3   Renminbi

15. The renminbi is the legal tender for all debts in China.
16. The unit of the renminbi is the Yuan.
17. Renminbi is to be printed and issued by the People's Bank of China only.
18. Illegally printing renminbi by any other person or organization is prohibited by law.
19. No organization or person can print or issue currency to replace the renminbi for circulation in the market.
20. Damaged renminbi notes can be exchanged in the offices of People's Bank of China for undamaged currency.
21. The People's Bank of China establishes an organization to print and manage renminbi.

Chapter 4   Daily functions

22. Monetary policy tools
    (i) Reserve ratio.
    (ii) Setting the basic and standard interest rates.
    (iii) Payment settlement for the financial firms which have accounts with the People's Bank of China.
    (iv) Discount loans to commercial banks.
    (v) Treasury notes and other government notes, management and sale, including foreign currency sale.
    (vi) Other monetary policy tools defined by the State Council.
23. Manage the state treasury.
24. Issue treasury notes and bonds.
25. Open accounts for financial firms. It is prohibited to overdraw funds from any particular account.
26. To manage a national clearance system between financial institutions.
27. To set the amount of discount loans, the discount rate and the duration.
28. The government cannot overdraw from its accounts at the People's Bank of China. The People's Bank of China cannot directly buy Treasury Bills at primary issue.

Box 3.9 (*continued*)

29. The People's Bank of China cannot provide loans to any local governments, or organizations. The People's Bank of China cannot provide guarantees to any organization or individual.

Chapter 5 Financial supervision

30. Supervise financial markets and assure that financial markets operate legally and stably.
31. The People's Bank of China is empowered to issue operating licences to financial firms.
32. The People's Bank of China has the right to audit the balance sheets of any financial firm at any time.
33. The People's Bank of China can order any other financial institution to provide their operating and balance sheet information, or other accounting information.
34. The People's Bank of China is authorized to produce and publish national statistical data.
35. The People's Bank of China shall direct and supervise the state policy banks.
36. The People's Bank of China shall have its own self-auditing system.

Chapter 6 Accounting

37. The People's Bank of China shall have an independent accounting budget management system.
38. The People's Bank of China must turn over its annual profit to the state, which equals revenue minus bank costs minus commercial bank reserves. A central bank loss shall be subsidized by the state.
39. The accounting and payment system of the People's Bank of China must be audited and supervised by the State Council.
40. The People's Bank of China shall create and publish a balance sheet and profit and loss statement and other accounting tables within three months after each accounting year. The People's Bank of China's accounting year shall start January 1st and end December 31st.

Source: ACFB (translated from Chinese version of *ACFB*, not reviewed by PBC. The author takes full responsibility for any translation errors.)

The 18 March legislation gave the People's Bank of China the essential tools of monetary policy, but the bank still needed to consolidate its role as regulator and supervisor of the commercial banks. To accomplish this additional legislation was introduced by the People's Congress on 10 May 1995, called 'The Commercial Banks Act of PRC'. The purpose of the legislation is not only to encourage the process of sound financial intermediation, but to formalize the process by law, and to strengthen the monetary policy transmission channel. The complete translation of the text of this legislation is presented in an Appendix, with excerpts discussed below.

Regarding the role of the banks as financial intermediaries, several important provisions are included in the 10 May legislation. Chapter 3 Article 29 stipulates that a commercial bank's private savings deposit business shall be conducted in accordance with the desires of their depositors, allowing depositors to withdraw their deposits on demand, paying interest on savings deposits, and protecting the privacy of depositors. Regarding loan quality, Chapter 1 Article 4 stipulates that commercial banks must assume responsibility for risk of loss, profitability, safety and liquidity, and manage themselves independently (from The People's Bank of China). Commercial banks shall do business according to the law without any interference from any person or organization. Commercial banks shall independently take legal responsibility in lawsuits. Moreover, Article 7 of Chapter 1 also mandates that commercial bank loans must be made in accordance with the creditworthiness of borrowers and the banks must do their best to make sure that loans can be repaid. To promote this end, Chapter 4 Article 37 mandates that commercial bank loans must be formalized in a loan contract. The loan contracts shall specify the loan type, loan usage, amount, interest rate, repayment date, and the responsibilities of both parties in the case of loan default. And Article 35 of Chapter 4 stipulates that the commercial banks shall monitor the borrower's use of funds, repayment ability, and repayment methods. In addition, to prevent conflicts of interest, the bank's office responsible for issuing loans shall be separated from the bank's office that originates the loan decisions.

The legislation also makes provisions for formalizing the supervisory and regulatory relation between the central bank (the People's Bank of China) and the commercial banks. Chapter 1 Article 10 states that the commercial banks shall be supervised by the People's Bank of China. Article 18 of Chapter 2 stipulates that the commercial banks shall have an audit committee consisting of representatives from the People's Bank of China, the central government, regulatory organizations and the bank itself. The audit committee is empowered to audit the banks' loan quality, balance sheet, state assets and management, and to prevent the bank from conducting illegal operations. Also, to promote disclosure and transparency, Article 28 of Chapter 2 requires public disclosure of major shareholders. Shareholders who want to buy more than 10 per cent of the commercial bank shares must apply for approval from the People's Bank of China, and under the provisions of Chapter 2 Article 15 section (v), the bank must submit to the People's Bank of China the credit history for each of its major shareholders.

To reinforce the 'firewall' provisions published in June 1993, that separate commercial banking from investment banking and other financial services, the 10 May 1995 legislation includes several clarifying provisions. Chapter 4 Article 43 stipulates that commercial banks cannot engage in trust and investment activity inside the borders of the People's Republic of China, and that they must not invest in real estate that is not occupied by the commercial bank itself. These provisions are reinforced in Chapter 8 Article 74 sections (iii) and (iv), which also prohibit the commercial banks from investing in non-bank financial firms and industrial enterprises. Moreover, in a related provision reminiscent of the Regulation Q provision of the US Glass-Steagall Act of 1933, Article 47 of Chapter 4 stipulates that commercial banks are prohibited from attracting savings deposits by manipulating interest rates. One recalls that the reason why Regulation Q was included in the Glass-Steagall Act was to prevent the kind of excessive interest-rate competition engaged in by US banks to attract depositors in the 1920s. US banks invested in low quality high-risk investments, many of which failed. To attract depositors, bankers bid up deposit interest rates to very high levels, undermining the banks and economy. Such provisions set the US banking system on a sound footing at the time, and apparently the lesson was not lost on the Chinese leadership when the time came to reform the financial architecture in the PRC in the mid-1990s.

Regarding the strengthening of the tools and procedures for the conduct of monetary policy, the 10 May 1995 legislation has several important provisions. First, Chapter 3 Article 31 and Chapter 4 Article 38 require the commercial banks to set interest rates to conform with the allowable rate established by the PBC. This allowed the central bank to use interest-rate targeting as a viable tool of monetary policy.

Second, the commercial banks are required to hold a fraction (13 per cent in 1980s) of their total assets in the form of cash reserves with the PBC under Article 32 of Chapter 3. Although not a true fractional reserve banking system, the PBC could use this arrangement, if it so chose, to regulate the level of credit in the banking system by manipulating the discount rate and controlling the level of commercial bank borrowing.

Moreover, the banks were allowed to make inter-bank loans to meet these reserve requirements under Article 3 Section (viii) of Chapter 1, setting up a kind of federal funds market. But commercial banks already had the ability to borrow from the PBC at interest, from previous legislation. In addition, the PBC began to set the stage for the use of open market operations as a tool of monetary policy. Chapter 1 Article 3 section (vi) designates the commercial banks as the government's agency to issue treasury bills, treasury notes, and treasury bonds to the public. Moreover, the banks are given permission to buy and sell treasury bills, notes and bonds for their own accounts. This is designed to lead to the development of a liquid treasury market for the central bank to eventually intervene in as a tool of monetary policy.

Financial data show the changes brought about by legislation. The PBC Act defined the PBC daily functions as using monetary policy tools such as the reserve ratio, and providing discount loans to commercial banks. Table 3.8 shows that discount loans to banks increased rapidly after 1995. In 1996 it increased 26 per cent to 1451.84. From Table 3.8, we can see that savings from other public organizations ceased in 1994 before the 18 March legislation. This is a step towards setting up the PBC as the central bank. It should not accept savings from public organizations as a specialized bank does. PBC liabilities to foreign financial firms stopped in 1994. The business was handed over to the BOC. All data show that, since 1994, the commercial banking and central banking functions were separated. The PBC became an independent central bank, relatively free from the government's political interference.

As discussed earlier, the PBC increased interest rates in 1993 in an effort to curb high inflation, but inflation continued. Then, in 1995, the bank tried again to curb inflation by raising the discount rate still further. On 1 January the bank raised the discount rate another 27 basis points to 10.89 per cent, and on 1 July it raised the discount rate another 27 basis points to 11.16 per cent. The reason for the odd number of basis points in each increase, is that once the central bank has decided to raise the discount rate, how much the rise will be is determined by how much additional revenue the bank needs to collect from outstanding discount loans to finance the costs of the banks' outstanding 'policy loans' (loans the central bank makes to subsidize unprofitable government-controlled sectors, such as agriculture, import-export, public investment in infrastructure). The bank also increased the fixed-asset investment rate (the long-term rate, greater than

Table 3.8 Balance sheet of PBC, the central bank of China (billion Yuan)

	1990	1991	1992	1993	1994	1995	1996	1997
Asset								
Loan	555.44	644.09	751.52	1058.08	1144.92			
to financial firms	514.77	599.18	698.13	989.85	1072.09			
to banks	509.07	591.88	678.02	962.57	1045.10	1151.00	1451.84	1435.79
to non-bank financial institutions	5.70	7.37	20.11	27.28	26.99	18.16	11.77	207.23
other loans	40.67	44.91	53.39	68.23	72.83			
Gold/foreign currency	61.15	124.01	111.39	88.75	427.59			
gold	1.20	1.20	1.20	1.20	1.20	1.20	1.20	1.20
foreign currency	59.95	122.81	110.19	87.55	426.39	651.1	933.00	1264.93
Asset in foreign banks	25.90	26.20	29.84	33.68	17.54	14.61	22.02	56.79
Borrowed	80.11	106.78	124.11	158.21				
Total	722.60	901.08	1016.8	1338.72				
Liability								
Savings	99.52	123.86	91.81	120.04	186.56	251.3	309.88	353.68
Treasury Dept	38.04	48.58	23.06	48.73	83.33	97.34	122.54	148.59
public organizations	61.48	75.28	68.75	71.31				
other savings	18.99	32.55	48.88	62.98				
Liability – financial firms	280.52	384.13	396.66	554.11	746.83	967.25	1435.49	1611.49
Reserve	139.06	180.98	233.54	288.46	396.12	524.65	761.24	924.87
Extra reserve	141.46	203.15	163.12	265.65	350.71	442.6	674.25	686.62
Currency issuing	278.82	333.63	457.45	628.76	788.39	857.4	943.48	1098.11
Liability – foreign firms	18.57	18.47	21.72	21.72				
Bank capital	29.15	34.53	50.86	66.40	26.57	37.11	36.68	36.62
Bonds						19.71	0	11.89
Other liability	-2.97	-26.09	-50.52	-115.29	-72.86	-167.7	-204.09	-119.06
Total	722.60	901.08	1016.86	1338.72				

Source: People's Bank of China, ACFB: *Almanac of China's Finance and Banking*, 1998.,

five years) on 1 January 1995 by 72 basis points, from 10.98 per cent to 11.7 per cent, in an effort to restrict credit and discourage long-term investment to slow down the economy. Then on 1 July 1995 the bank also increased the working-capital loan rate (the short-term rate, less than one year) 108 basis points from 10.98 per cent to 12.06 per cent.

3.7 Development of the money market and the 1996–7 reforms

The money market in the PRC includes the inter-bank lending market, the central bank's discount window, and the treasury bill market. The money market plays a key role in the central bank's open market operations. The PBC reinforced the development of the money market for the purpose of future open market operations.

The inter-bank lending market

The inter-bank lending market is the core component of the currency market. In the inter-bank lending market, financial institutions conduct short-term dynamic borrowing. It covers the short-term demands of financial institutions in capital shortage when making large payments. The Chinese inter-bank lending market was officially approved by the PBC in October 1984 in order to end the previous vertical management of credit allocation by the PBC. Around 1993, many financial institutions treated inter-bank lending as a long-term commitment for investment in real estate and caused chaos in the inter-bank lending market, partially contributing to the 1993 inflation (Duo Xie, 2001).

In January 1996 the PBC began to set up the nation-wide inter-bank lending market. Four state-owned commercial banks and their branches and city commercial banks are its members. They trade directly through the electronic network system in the National Inter-bank Lending Centre. All other non-member financial institutions participate in trading in the local areas and report to the PBC. In June 1996 the PBC allowed the inter-bank lending rates to be decided by financial institutions. In 1998 the PBC gave licences to 33 city commercial banks, 9 foreign banks and 10 insurance companies to allow them to join the inter-bank market. At the end of 1998 the total number of inter-bank trading institutions was 177 compared with the 61 members at the end of 1997. 'The Inter-bank Trading Rules', 'The Rules for Clearance between Banks' and the 'Regulations for the Policy Bank Issue of Bonds' were legislated in 1998. The PBC increased the monetary policy instruments by allowing three bonds to enter the federal fund market: the policy banks' bonds issued in 1998, the special government bonds of 45 billion RMB and the construction bonds of 70 billion issued by the Treasury Department of the State Council.

The PBC restricts the maturation time limit of inter-bank lending to less than four months and the borrowing amount to be dependent on net deposits. The electronic network dynamically provides trading information to the PBC and is very important for the PBC to monitor and control market fluctuation.

Since its inception, the inter-bank lending market has developed quickly. In March 1989 inter-bank transactions in 11 Chinese cities totalled 352.9 million Yuan RMB, at interest rates of 10.44 per cent to 14.0 per cent (Bank of Tokyo, 1994). In 1999 the average monthly trading volume was 28 billion Yuan RMB and was 56 billion Yuan RMB in 2000 (Duo Xie, 2001). The PBC was aware of the long-existing Chinese tradition of a high capital reserve ratio which made the commercial banks reluctant to do inter-bank lending. It somehow restricted the development of the money market. In June 1996, PBC allowed banks to decide rates of inter-bank lending by themselves. It boosted the inter-bank lending market in 1996–7. Before June 1997 the commercial banks traded treasury bills and government bonds through stockbrokers, which might cause the commercial banks' funds to enter the stock markets. Starting from June 1997, PBC's new policy prevents commercial banks' funds from flowing into stock brokerage firms to trade treasury bills. In 1998 the trading quantity dropped to 25 per cent of that in 1997 (Table 3.9). However, things changed after 2001 when the inter-bank lending rate dropped from 2.62 per cent in January 2001 to 2.39 per cent in September 2001 due to the deflation effect. In addition, the inter-bank lending market was stimulated by the securities firms and the investment fund managers who borrowed 400 billion Yuan RMB in 2001, 77.1 per cent more than the previous year. In the first nine months of 2001, total inter-bank lending was 3.31 trillion Yuan RMB, increased by 1.92 trillion compared with the same period the previous year, as shown in Table 3.9.

There are more trading items in the money market. In 1997, lending with a maturation period of seven days or less (including overnight) was 32.65 per cent (6.5 plus 26.15 in Table 3.10) of the total trading amount. And in 2000 it increased to 71.4 per cent (7.7 plus 63.7 per cent in Table 3.10). Compared with 1993, when inter-bank lending was treated as the funds for long-term investment, this figure shows that the inter-bank lending market in China is converging to the international market standard with emphasis on the adjustment of bank capital shortage in the short term.

Table 3.9 Total annual trading quantity of currency markets (billion Yuan RMB)

Year	Inter-bank lending	Treasury bill market
1997	829.8*	30.7
1998	197.8	102.1
1999	329.1	394.9
2000	672.8	1578.2
2001 (January	600.8	2672.2
to September)	(increase by 32.7 per cent)	(increase by 69.3 per cent)

*The big number here reflected the policy change. Before June 1997 the commercial banks traded treasury bills and government bonds through stockbrokers. It produced a loophole for banking funds to enter the stock markets. Starting from June 1997, PBC's new policy prevents commercial banks funds flowing into stock brokerage firms to trade in treasury bills.
Sources: D. Xie, 2001; Wenhong Zhang, 2001.

Table 3.10 Inter-bank lending market trade distribution according to maturation period (%)

	Overnight	<7 days	8–20 days	21–30 days	31–60 days	61–90 days	91–120 days
1997	6.5	26.15	10.63	13.74	23.14	12.91	6.93
1998	6	22.5	14.5	22.6	18.3	10.5	5.6
1999	10.9	28.6	7.4	21.2	27.9	3.3	0.7
2000	7.7	63.7	12	4.9	9.2	2.3	0.1

Source: Chinese Inter-bank Lending Center; D. Xie, 2001.

In the late 1990s the PBC built the electronic trading network for inter-bank lending. The PBC allowed licensed security firms, insurance companies, fund management companies and financial corporations to enter the inter-bank lending market. The PBC also allowed state-owned commercial banks to act as agents of small financial firms to undertake inter-bank lending business. Direct borrowing from the PBC was no longer allowed. The PBC intends to initiate open market operations with government bonds. Short-term bonds were issued partly as a means of preparing for effective open market operations. However, the market value of treasury bills was smaller than that of the inter-bank lending market. The effect of these operations in conducting monetary control was very limited.

To further stimulate the development of the inter-bank lending market, the PBC decreased the inter-bank lending rate 430 basis points in 1998. It changed from 8.7 per cent in January 1998, and was down to 4.5 per cent in December 1998. The average rate for the PBC to buy back treasury bills was 5.661 per cent in 1998, a decrease of 335 basis points. The range was from 8.66 per cent in January 1998 to 4.26 per cent in

December 1998. The reason for the decrease is that the PBC eased the benchmark rates three times during the year.

The rates for different inter-bank lending instruments showed big differences. The short-term rate was higher than the long-term rate because of the prediction of lower interest rates in the long run.

The trade volume of inter-bank lending decreased by 76.15 per cent to 98.9 billion RMB. It showed volume variation from month to month. The range was from the highest 11.9 billion in January to the lowest 2.27 billion in May 1998. The main reason of decrease was the preparation for more reserves for trade risks, emphasizing safe trading.

Treasury bill markets

Treasury bills have the function of macro-regulation of the economy. Government executes active fiscal policy by using treasury bills to increase public consumption and to stimulate domestic demand.

The discounting, acceptance and rediscounting of treasury bills started in Shanghai in 1980 and was formally approved by the PBC in December 1984. A second market for trading treasury bills existed in seven cities in 1989 (Shenzhen, Guangzhou, Shenyang, Shanghai, Harbin, Wuhan and Chongqing). An experimental placement of government bonds through underwriting syndicates brought success in April 1991. Since then treasury bills and government bonds have usually been sold through such syndicates. Compulsory sales of government bonds were reintroduced in 1993, when stocks and corporate bonds offered higher yields. In 1994 the Chinese government took steps to finance the budget deficit by issuing bonds in both domestic and international financial markets (Bank of Tokyo, 1994).

Before 1997 the treasury bill market was only a small proportion of the market, which then mainly focused on inter-bank lending. As the risk management concept has entered commercial bank management, the treasury bill market has developed quickly in recent years. The participants in the treasury bill markets include state-owned commercial banks, other commercial banks, foreign bank branches in China, insurance companies, securities firms, fund management companies and the rural trust companies. The total assets of those participants are 95 per cent of the total assets of Chinese financial institutions. This represents more participation than the inter-bank lending market. Not only was the initial issue of treasury bills successful, but also the secondary market of trading treasury bills. Total volume of secondary trading in 1998 was 2299 billion Yuan RMB, an increase of 38.95 per cent compared with 1997. The PBC decreased the interest rate seven times from

1996 to 1999 and the commercial banks and other financial corporations prefer to put money in the safe harbour of treasury bills. These are the reasons pushing the secondary treasury bill market up. The risks of trading treasury bills are lower than inter-bank lending.

The trade of treasury bills gradually moved to the Shanghai Stock Exchange. Shanghai Stock Exchange had the biggest volume of trading, which was 93 per cent of the total treasury bill trade volume.

Importance of the treasury bill market

The development of the treasury bill market helped the process by which the treasury bill rate and yield are decided by the financial markets. The formation of the yield structure provides an important clue for the PBC to study the trend of future inflation. It also provides a reference for the pricing of the other financial products.

In addition, the development of the treasury bill market makes it convenient for commercial banks to adjust their capital reserve in order to decrease the extra capital reserve and use the fund more efficiently.

Treasury bills are becoming a bigger and bigger proportion of bank assets. For example, in 2001 the PBC conducted open market operations many times, and traded in M0 net value 1886.6 billion Yuan RMB. Open market operations regulated the interest rates in the currency market. In 2001 the open market operation rates became the benchmark rates.

The PBC uses the discount loan to support small enterprises. By the end of August 2001, discount loans totalled 108.6 billion Yuan RMB. Most of them went to small financial institutions.

1996–7 reforms

In 1996 the PBC focused on interest-rate targets and reserve ratio requirements in its conduct of monetary policy, but had to quickly abandon open market operations because of the immaturity of the Chinese treasury market. The treasury market was simply too thin and shallow. Because the high inflation the PRC had experienced since 1993 had abated, the central bank embarked on an expansionary monetary policy regime in an effort to stimulate economic growth. M1 and M2 rose steadily from 1996 to 1998, and the discount rate on member bank borrowing was successively lowered from 10.44 per cent in 1996, and 9.00 per cent in 1997 to 5.22 per cent by 1998, to stimulate discount borrowing. At the same time, the central bank lowered the interest rate paid on reserves held by the central bank for member banks to discourage member banks from holding excess reserves with the central bank. The rate paid on these reserves was successively lowered from 9.18 per cent on 1 July 1995, to 8.82 per cent on 1 May

1996, to 8.28 per cent on 23 August 1996, and then to 7.56 per cent on 23 October 1997. It finally reached 2.07 per cent on 6 October 1999. Reserve ratio requirements were stabilized at 13 per cent of total deposits through 1998, the same rate it had been since 1988. During this period, China also maintained a fixed-exchange-rate regime, pegging the renminbi to the US dollar at a rate of 8.3 Yuan per US dollar. This rate had been maintained since 1993. Table 3.11 summarizes the conduct and consequences of monetary policy in China for the period 1996 to 1998.

To further strengthen the central bank's control over monetary policy, the PBC announced several changes in its conduct of monetary policy after its 1 June 1996 board meeting. The central bank changed its focus away from interest-rate targets towards money supply targets, and began to test its ability to control M1 and M2 through open market operations. Open market operations did not however start to become a serious monetary policy tool in China until the end of 1999, when the Chinese treasury market became more liquid (*Financial Times*, 6 January 2000). Box 3.10 is a translation of the announcement of the PBC minutes of its 1 June 1996 meeting.

Box 3.10   Announcement of the People's Bank of China board meeting 1 June 1996

1. Monetary policy will now be conducted through money supply control and supervision. Credit control through interest rate targeting will no longer be the primary policy objective of the central bank. M1 and M2 will now be the central bank's operating targets.
2. To improve the efficiency of the loan management system, state-owned commercial banks shall be managed according to their balance sheets. The People's Bank of China shall give commercial banks loan quota earlier than previously scheduled to enable commercial banks to balance their loan business throughout the whole year.
3. The central bank shall maintain a stable money supply in the long run, but may alter the money supply in the short run in order to fine-tune the economy. In May and August of 1996 the People's Bank of China decreased benchmark interest rates twice, and helped state-owned enterprises to repay their loans more easily.
4. The central bank shall create an inter-bank system of borrowing and lending in order to facilitate the conduct of open market operations by the central bank. In 1996 the People's Bank of China tested open market operations by selling T-bills for the first time.

Table 3.11 Monetary policy in China, 1996–2001 (represented indicators) (billion of Yuan RMB)

Year	GDP, Nominal	M0 (billion Renminbi) (% growth)	M1 (billion Renminbi) (% growth)	M2 (billion Renminbi) (% growth)	Discount rate	CPI*	Exchange rate	Reserve Ratio (%)
1996	6685	880.2	2851 (16%)	7609.5 (23%)	10.08	106.1	8.29	13
1997	7314 (8.8%)	1017.8	3483 (18%)	9099.5 (16%)	8.64	100.8	8.29	13
1998	7697 (7.8%)	1120.4	3895 (6%)	10449.9 (12%)	6.39	100.2	8.29	8 (03/1998)
1999	8042 (7.1%)	1345.6	4583.7 (17.7%)	11989.8 (14.7%)	5.85	100.2	8.29	6 (11/1999)
2000	8940	1470	5300 (16%)	13460 (12.3%)	5.85	100.4	8.279	6
2001	N/A	1600	5900 (12.7%)	15800 (14.4%)	5.85	101.2	8.277	6

*CPI takes previous year data as 100.

Source: GDP data from PBC website on the Internet. The 2001 data from the Chinese Central TV Channel 4, 15 Jan. 2002. All the other data from the China Statistics Yearbook, various editions.

The difference between the Chinese banking system and that of the United States

According to Yang (1996), the control-oriented nature of the Chinese planning system placed the national banks in a less important position than the fiscal system. This avoided the systemic conflict within the economy. The so-called 'centralized economy' needed a centralized commercial banking system.

For the convenience of control, the centralised commercial banks were limited to certain businesses or sectors. For example, the Agriculture Bank mainly deals with rural and agricultural business. This is significantly different from those in the United States. It is understandable because all the major commercial banks are solely owned by the Chinese government.

3.8 Summary

Inflation in 1993 was tough for the Chinese economy. However, it forced the Chinese central bank to learn to use monetary tools such as interest rate control, which turned out to be effective: 'The strawberry grows underneath the nettle' (Shakespeare, *Henry V*. I. i. 60).

During the 1993 to 1997 period, controlling inflation was the task of 1993, easing foreign exchange rate restriction was the task of 1994–5, legislation for the central bank was the task for 1995, and the emphasis was on monetary policy in 1996. The year 1993 was a benchmark year in Chinese central banking, when modern-day central banking began in the PRC for the first time. The central bank recognized the importance of the interest-rate policy as a viable monetary policy tool, and began to use it as such in the conduct of monetary policy thereafter.

At this time, the PBC called the interest rate operation a reform, not a monetary policy tool. But the importance of the interest rate was weighted for the Chinese central bankers like Hongru Liu, vice-president of the PBC. He and colleagues developed a theory stating that lending rates cannot suddenly go higher than the inflation rate. Otherwise, the increased cost borne by enterprises will finally be transferred to consumers, causing the retail price to sharply increase.

In 1994–5 the foreign exchange rate restriction was eased. The monetary policy target was changed to maintenance of exchange rate stability. In response to this change, the PBC tested money supply as a tool to conduct open market operations in 1995. Because of the immaturity of the inter-bank lending market and the small size of the treasury bill market, open market operation ceased.

In 1995–7, the new policy approach introduced money supply targets and the manipulation of reserve ratio requirements as monetary policy tools. In addition, legislation was introduced to separate financial service operations, including insurance underwriting, from commercial banks to newly created securities corporations and insurance companies. Moreover, to professionalize the operations of the central bank, the policy loan management function of the central bank was spun off into three newly created Policy Banks: the Chinese Agriculture Development Bank, the State Development Bank and the Chinese Import Export Bank. This partially insulated the central bank from government policy interference by isolating it from the process of subsidizing the government-controlled sectors of the economy. The central bank could concentrate on regulating the monetary system in accordance with sound central banking practice, free of political pressure. In 1996–7 the PBC focused on interest-rate targets and reserve ratio requirements in its conduct of monetary policy, but had to quickly abandon open market operations because of the immaturity of the Chinese treasury market.

Following the 1993–7 reforms, the Chinese banking system was put on a sound financial footing. The new legislation, taken in total, separated out the policy banks from the commercial banks, reducing the pressures for state-directed credit. The commercial banks were separated from the central bank, facilitating sound financial intermediation and reinforcing bank supervision and regulatory control. In addition, the PBC was given a clear monetary policy role, and the tools to implement this role, such as exclusive control over the setting of interest rates, reserve ratio requirements, the creation of an inter-bank money market, and the implementation of open market operations. Moreover, to prevent conflicts of interest, commercial banking operations were separated from investment banking operations in separate banks, instituting the same kind of firewalls as the US Glass-Steagall Act of 1933.

4
The Asian Financial Crisis and Chinese Banking Reforms in 1998–2001

'He must have a long spoon that must eat with the devil.'

William Shakespeare, *The Comedy of Errors*, IV. iii. 65

4.1 The Asian Financial Crisis of 1997

On 2 July 1997 the Asian Financial Crisis officially began with the devaluation of the Thai baht by 15–20 per cent. For Thailand, Indonesia, South Korea and Malaysia, the much-celebrated 'Asian Economic Miracle' came to an abrupt end. After decades of fast-paced growth and virtually uninterrupted expansion, there had been an abrupt reversal in capital flows out of these East Asian economies as growth prospects soured after the boom turned to bust. Much of the hot capital flowing into these countries in the years leading up to the crisis had turned from long-term foreign direct investment to short-term speculative investment, which was unsustainable in the long run. Much of the capital flowed in to finance an East Asian real estate bubble, which eventually collapsed, causing a deflation in asset prices. These countries saw their financial systems collapse, their economies falter and millions of their citizens returned to poverty, all within a few months. The financial crisis spread quickly to the Philippines and Hong Kong, then to Brazil and Russia, and eventually to Japan.

In 1993 the World Bank published 'The East Asian Miracle: Economic Growth and Public Policy (World Bank, 1993)'. The bank reported that for most of the three prior decades, the East Asian 'tigers', with South Korea as the leader of the pack, and the 'Newly Industrializing Economies' – Indonesia, Malaysia and Thailand – had generated increases in gross domestic product at the unprecedented rate of 5 per cent to 7 per cent annually. Questions were raised about whether the 'miracle' was genuine in terms of having achieved a shift in productivity or whether it was simply the result of pouring more resources into these economies. Yet the benefits were tangible. An estimated 350 million East Asians had been lifted out of poverty. It appeared that the countries had broken out of the poverty trap and had entered the ranks of dynamic and self-sustaining economies (Arestis and Demetriades, 1999).

Then, the growth came to an abrupt end. During 1997 and 1998 South Korea, Thailand, Malaysia, Indonesia and other Asian countries experienced various degrees of financial and economic collapse. Lots of banks and corporations have gone bankrupt, per capita income has plunged, and billions in savings have evaporated. Millions of jobs were lost. The collapse spread further through Asia and in other areas of the global economy remains very much alive.

However, China remained relatively insulated from the contagion. Chinese monetary policy played an active role in protecting China from the crisis, stimulating economic growth and finally helping the PRC to recover from the export drop effected by the crisis. The major characteristics of this monetary policy were keeping a low interest rate and stabilizing the exchange rate, stimulating government bond sales, stimulating consumption, stimulating investment and capital market development, increasing the foreign exchange reserve and maintaining the Chinese trade balance. As we saw in Table 3.11 (p. 83), the Chinese were able to maintain a stable exchange rate of 8.29RMB/$ through 1998, and real GDP actually grew through the period.

What's more, it appears that China was never in danger of having a collapsing currency throughout the crisis. As we can see from Table 4.1, China's reserve position remained strong throughout the period, growing consistently from the second quarter of 1997 through to the second quarter of 1998 (and is still growing). By contrast, we observe that Indonesian, Korean, Malaysian and Thai reserves all began to fall dramatically. Indonesian reserves fell from $20,336 million in the second quarter of 1997 to $15,770 million by the first quarter of 1998 when the trend began to reverse. Korean reserves fell from $34,070 million in the second quarter of 1997 to $20,367 million by the 4th quarter of 1997, when reserves bottomed out. Malaysian reserves dropped from $26,865 million in the second quarter of 1997 to $19,702 million in the second quarter of 1998, when its reserve position trend began to reverse. Thai reserves dropped from $31,361 million in the second quarter of 1997 to $25,785 million by the second quarter of 1998, when its reserve position trend began to reverse.

Table 4.1 Total reserve minus gold (millions of US dollars)

Year. Quarter	PRC	Indonesia	Japan	Korea	Malaysia	Thailand
1996.1	82 701	4953	202 712	3418	23 508	37 938
1996.2	88 606	15 579	208 978	36 527	25 542	38 787
1996.3	97 362	15 490	213 810	32 829	26 071	38 494
1996.4	107 039	18 251	216 648	34 037	27 009	37 731
1997.1	113 962	19 012	218 181	29 893	27 710	37 074
1997.2	122 825	20 336	221 128	34 070	26 586	31 361
1997.3	136 024	20 275	224 412	30 389	22 159	28 622
1997.4	142 762	16 587	219 640	20 367	20 788	26 179
1998.1	143 982	15 770	222 460	29 683	19 804	26 893
1998.2	143 957	17 950	204 745	40 835	19 702	25 785
1998.3	145 016	19 650	211 163	46 912	20 702	26 578
1998.4	149 188	22 713	215 471	51 975	25 559	28 825
1999.1	150 497	25 161	221 371	57 385	27 140	29 230
1999.2	150 565	26 319	245 245	61 920	30 571	30 723
1999.3	154 731	26 032	271 194	65 415	31 134	31 649
1999.4	157 728	26 445	286 916	73 987	30 588	34 063

Source: *International Financial Statistics*, 2000.

Short-term interest rates and foreign investment

In addition, short-term interest rates also tell an interesting tale. Table 4.2 shows the short-term interest rate trends during the period of the crisis for the PRC, Indonesia, Japan, Korea, Malaysia and Thailand. The Chinese short-term rate, their discount rate on member bank borrowing, remained constant at 9 per cent from the second quarter of 1997 through the third quarter of 1997, and then dropped to 8.55 per cent in the fourth quarter of 1997, and continued to drop slowly thereafter through 1999. By contrast the Indonesian short-term rate rose from 10.5 per cent in the second quarter of 1997 to 22 per cent by the third quarter of 1997, and then rose dramatically through the third quarter of 1998, when it reached a high of 68.76 per cent. The Thai short-term rate also rose, but less, from 10.5 per cent in the second quarter of 1997 to 12.5 per cent in the third quarter of 1997, and remained there through the fourth quarter of 1998. Korean and Malaysian short-term rates remained constant throughout the period of the crisis, their central banks apparently preferring to use exchange intervention as a tool to stabilize their currencies, as opposed to contractionary monetary policy, in an attempt to reverse capital outflows.

Table 4.2 Short-term interest rate (discount rate per cent)

Year. Quarter	PRC	Indonesia	Japan	Korea	Malaysia	Thailand
1996.1	10.44	13.99	0.50	5	7.0	10.5
1996.2	9	13.99	0.5	5	7.1	10.5
1996.3	9	13.96	0.5	5	7.0	10.5
1996.4	9	12.80	0.5	5	7.28	10.5
1997.1	9	11.07	0.5	5	7.28	10.5
1997.2	9	10.50	0.5	5	7.28	10.5
1997.3	9	22.00	0.5	5	7.28	12.5
1997.4	8.55	20.00	0.5	5	7.28	12.5
1998.1	6.39	27.75	0.5	5	7.28	12.5
1998.2	6.39	58.00	0.5	5	7.28	12.5
1998.3	5.22	68.76	0.5	3	7.28	12.5
1998.4	5.22	38.44	0.5	3	7.28	12.5
1999.1	4.59	37.84	0.5	3	7.28	7.0
1999.2	4.59	22.05	0.5	3	7.28	5.5
1999.3	3.24	13.02	0.5	3	7.28	4.0
1999.4	3.24	12.51	0.5	3	7.28	4.0

Source: *International Financial Statistics*, 2000.

Table 4.2 also shows that, in January 1996, the short-term interest rates in Indonesia, Malaysia and Thailand were 13.99, 7.0 and 10.5 per cent respectively. But at the same time, in the United States and Japan, short-term interest rates were less than 4 per cent and 1 per cent respectively. The short-term interest rates of these East Asian countries were much higher than those in Western countries. Due to the currency pegging to the US dollar, financial institutions from all over the world gradually piled up what they considered to be risk-free, high-yielding loans. At the same time, domestic banks, start-up financial institutions, corporations and a variety of other private intermediaries in these Asian countries found that they could borrow capital more cheaply and more readily abroad than they could borrow at home. Moreover, the governments in those Asian countries except China opened the market to foreign financial markets in the 1980s and early 1990s (Katz, 1999). For example, in the mid-1990s according to Table 4.2, an Asian investor could borrow Japanese yen at nearly zero interest to invest in a bank in Indonesia and expect to earn a more than 10 per cent annual return.

In 1996 and 1997 there were few opportunities to make profitable investment because of the previous 10–20 years of high-speed development in East Asian countries. But capital inflow still kept rising. By 1996 annual net private capital inflows to four East Asian countries had been $109 billion. It was 11 per cent of the GDP of those East Asian Countries. All of those capital inflows were invested on highly risky projects.

China also had a high short-term interest rate, which was 10.44 in January 1996. But China did not open its financial markets to foreign investors until December of 2001 when it successfully joined the World Trade Organization. When foreign loans piled up in the East Asian countries, with their economies on the edge of collapse in early 1997, foreign banks in China were not even allowed to freely exchange the local currency renminbi (RMB), not to mention operating RMB deposits and loans. This is the reason why China was able to avoid the Asian Financial Crisis even though the Chinese short-term interest rates were almost as high as the other East Asian countries. South Korea had a low short-term interest rate, which was 5 per cent in January 1996. But it was still significantly higher than that of Japan (less than 1 per cent at the same time). Considering the opened foreign loan markets and pegging of the local currency (Won) to the US dollars, it is not hard to understand why South Korea could not survive the crisis.

But in China, the overheated economy had already been soft-landed from 1993–5, due to the central banking reform during this period, and had much less exposure to high risk investment. Moreover, foreign investment never plays a major role in the bread-and-butter industries, which are operated by SOEs.

The state-owned enterprises: a buffer to insulate China from crisis

In 1980 the SOEs produced 75 per cent of industrial output, collectively owned firms 24 per cent, and other private or shareholding companies 1 per cent. The Chinese SOEs functioned as passive agents of the state economic bureaucracy. Managers had little authority over research and development, product innovation, investment planning, marketing, or even such routine matters as production scheduling, material purchases, wage structures and employment levels, before the start of the Chinese industry reform in 1980.

By 1992 the SOEs produced 48 per cent of industrial output, collectively owned firms' production increased to 38 per cent, and other private or shareholding companies 14 per cent. The SOEs are always supervised by central government or local government. They are not allowed to let foreign investment dominate the enterprises (today, China still refuses the idea that foreign investment can hold more than 50 per cent shares of SOEs) and agriculture (which is still largely based on family operation and far away from accepting foreign investment). The state has better control over the management of SOEs than

Table 4.3 Consumer price index: comparison of Asian countries(%)

Year. Quarter	Korea	Indonesia	PRC	Malaysia	Thailand
1996.1	103.0	107.1	9.4	102.4	104.0
1996.2	104.7	107.6	9.1	103.2	105.2
1996.3	105.8	108.1	7.9	103.9	106.3
1996.4	106.2	109.1	7.0	104.5	107.7
1997.1	107.8	112.2	5.2	105.6	108.6
1997.2	108.9	112.9	2.9	105.8	109.7
1997.3	110.0	116.2	2.1	106.3	112.9
1997.4	111.6	119.7	1.0	107.3	115.8
1998.1	117.5	142.7	N/A	110.2	118.4
1998.2	117.8	168.8	−0.9	111.8	121.1
1998.3	117.7	202.7	−1.4	112.3	122.1
1998.4	118.3	212.4	−1.1	113.1	121.5
1999.1	118.3	226.0	−1.4	114.5	121.6
1999.2	118.5	221.0	−2.1	114.8	120.5
1999.3	118.5	216.2	−1.3	114.9	120.9
1999.4	119.8	216.0	N/A	115.4	121.0

Source: *International Financial Statistics*, 2000.

other private or collective enterprises. The state encourages enterprises to be careful to take up new projects, especially real estate, and encourages them to hold more capital. All these reduced the potential losses for the state when the 1997 crisis hit. The increased cash level in enterprises is a cushion that makes enterprise bankruptcy less likely. So in mid-1997 when the financial crisis hit, China was immune to it.

4.2 Deflation and its positive and negative effects

Deflation

Since 1996, the retail price index (RPI) and the consumer price index in China have been decreasing. In October 1997 the retail price index dropped below zero to −0.4 per cent (Table 4.4). It has been negative till 2000 except for a few brief spikes above zero. For example, in March of 1998, the RPI briefly returned to a positive value of 0.7 per cent, which reflected the short-term consumer demand increase for food and transportation in the Chinese New Year. Then RPI became negative again, and did not increase until 2000.

From January to August 1998, the consumer price index (CPI) decreased by 0.6 percentage point when compared with the same time in the previous year. It is a sign of deflation.

Table 4.4 Retail price index tells a deflation story

	Oct. 1997	Feb. 1998	Mar. 1998	Aug. 1998
Retail price index	−0.4 per cent	−0.1 per cent	0.7 per cent	−0.4 per cent

Source: People's Bank of China, *ACFB: Almanac of China's Finance and Banking*, 1997–2000.

Savings deposit numbers also indicate deflation. In 1997 commercial banking savings deposits increased by 1294 billion Yuan RMB, which was 186 billion Yuan RMB less than the previous year. This was because some money was put into stock markets. Loans increased by 1070 billion Yuan RMB, which was 15.9 billion Yuan RMB less than that of last year.

In 1998 total savings were 10.3 trillion Yuan RMB, which was an increase of 1.4 trillion. This was only a 16.2 per cent increase (Table 4.5). When compared with the 22.4 per cent increase at the same time in 1997, the increase of deposits was significantly less. In 1998 total loans were 9.39 trillion in all banks, increasing by 1.15 trillion which was a 14 per cent increase.

The reduction in savings deposits should decrease the money supply because savings were one-third of the money supply M1. Data showed that the money supply slowed down in 1998. M1 growth in January 1998 was still strong and increased by 14.6 per cent. But it then started to decrease and, in June of 1998, M1 only increased by 8.7 per cent (*ACFB*, 1999). In 1998 M1 was 3,895 billion Yuan RMB, an increase of only 6 per cent, which was much smaller than the growth of 18 per cent in 1997 (Table 3.11, P. 83).

The reason that savings decreased in 1998 is as follows: the interest rates were reduced twice, and this discouraged savings; unemployment rate increased, and people had less money to save; the Asian Financial Crisis had a negative effect on export profits due to other Asian countries' cheaper goods.

Table 4.5 Savings deposits and loan statistics in 1997–9 show deflation (trillion Yuan)

Year	Savings	Increase of savings	Per cent increase of savings	Total loan	Increase of loans	Per cent increase of loans
1997	5.78	1.29	22.4		1.07	
1998	10.3	1.4	16.2	9.39	1.15	14

Source: People's Bank of China, *ACFB: Almanac of China's Finance and Banking*, 1997–2000.

Some people may ask this question. Are the maximum effects of deflation experienced in China? Deflation, which is the opposite of inflation, is defined as a continuous decrease in the money supply and in the prices of commodities and services. It is the currency presentation of economic retreat. When the GDP declines continuously in more than two consecutive quarters, economic recession accompanies deflation. Deflation has three features: first, the price keeps falling and money supply keeps falling. Second, demand decreases and the unemployment rate is high. Third, economy enters recession and the GDP decreases.

The decrease of money supply and prices in the PRC in 1998–2000 did not fully explain deflation. Even though the rate of increase of the money supply slowed, the money supply was still growing. The decrease of prices did not affect the Chinese economy very much. GDP growth rate was still 7.8 per cent per year in 1998.

Deflation has positive effects in China. After the 1997 Asian Financial Crisis, the Chinese currency RMB was subjected to deflationary pressure. International hedge funds attacked Hong Kong currency in October 1997. At the same time, the Chinese CPI coincidently turned negative. It was a big support to the exchange rate of Chinese and Hong Kong currency. It was perfect timing: RMB kept its promise to the foreign exchange markets and it beat hedge fund speculation that RMB would deflate. This was a significant contribution to the Asian economic recovery after the crisis.

4.3 Banking reform since 1997

In 1997–9 the Chinese export industry had competition from Asian countries which had deflated currency and a favoured situation in the export markets. In this period, a deflation situation was gradually developing in China. Retail prices and consumer prices decreased. Enterprise profits decreased and the unemployment rate increased. Monetary policy in this period focused on the stimulation of economic growth and the control of deflation.

The 1997 Asian Financial Crisis caused the currency devaluation of other Asian countries, while Chinese currency still maintained its value. The cheap export prices made it easier for other Asian countries to export goods. Chinese export quantities dropped due to the competition from those countries. In order to stimulate exports, the Chinese central bank changed monetary policy after 1997. In 1997–8, the Chinese monetary policy was to ensure the good quality of loans and prevent financial risks, and to support the economy's rapid growth.

For example, the PBC pre-set the target for monetary policy: the GDP growth target was set at 8 per cent, the inflation target was set equal to the consumer price index (4 to 5 per cent). The money supply increase target was 14–15 per cent. This was a proper increase in the money supply. When conducting monetary policy in 1998, the central bank actively increased credit and loans, and reduced interest rates.

In 1998 the system construction and functionality of the discount window was improved. The PBC reformed the discount rate system and treated it as a benchmark rate, separating it from the loan rate. In 1997–9, the PBC used the discount rate as the monetary policy tool. The discount rate was decreased from 10.62 per cent in September 1997 to 3.78 per cent in June 1999 (Table 4.6).

The rate cuts in 1997–9 increased consumption, investment and exports. The GDP growth in 1998 was 7.8 per cent. This was in the face of both deflation and the export decrease.

PBC's active rate cuts prepare the money market for the open market operation. The open market operation was the central bank's policy tool. In order to effectively manage the M0 (base money) and ensure the money supply for financial institutions, the PBC re-established the open market operation by trading treasury bills on 26 May 1998. In the second half of 1998 the PBC had a total of 36 open market operations. Total treasury bills bought were 176.1 billion RMB, monetary supply 70.1 billion RMB. The number of the initial traders increased to 28 companies. The instruments used in trade, securities' maturation period and type increased dramatically. It was the important way for the PBC to manage money supply. The open market operations were active, flexible, timely and fair. The necessary tools were created to execute monetary policy in the open market operations. Both monetary policy and fiscal policy were used simultaneously.

The Chinese currency RMB maitained a stable exchange rate after the Asian Financial Crisis. The reasons are as follows:

1. GDP experienced significant growth of 7.8 per cent in 1998, which was responsible for the stability of the Chinese currency. The world average GDP growth rate was only 2 per cent that was substantially less than the Chinese GDP. The retail price index dropped 260 basis points, the consumer price index dropped by 80 basis points. The GDP growth rate was significant and both price indices were low. These were solid supports for the maintenance of a stable currency exchange rate.

Table 4.6 The PBC discount rate to the commercial banks and the commercial banks loan rate in 1990–9

Year Month/date*	1990 8/21	1991 4/21	1993 4/1	1993 5/15	1993 7/11	1995 1/1	1995 7/1	1996 5/1	1996 8/23	1997 10/23	1998 3/25	1998 7/1	1998 12/7	1999 6/10	2002 2/20
PBC discount loan rate	7.92	7.2	7.38	9.0	10.62	10.89	11.16	10.98	10.62	9.36	7.92	5.67	5.13	3.78	
Commercial bank loan rate	9.36	8.64	N/A	9.36	10.98	10.98	12.06	10.98	10.08	8.64	7.92	6.93	6.39	5.85	5.31

* indicates month and date when PBC change the rates.
Source: Interest Rates Brochure, PBC Wuhan Branch, June 1999.

2. China had a significant surplus in international trade. It was the guarantee of the stability of the Chinese currency's exchange rate. The policies which the Chinese government implemented were successful. In 1998 total exports were US$183.76 billion, which was an increase of 0.5 per cent; the trade surplus was US$43.59 billion, which was slightly higher than that of the previous year. New investments from foreign companies were US$52.13 billion, which was an increase of 2.21 per cent.

3. China had US$145 billion in foreign exchange reserves in autumn 1998, which was equal to one year's import payments. Sufficient foreign exchange reserve is the solid support for the stability of the exchange rate. It increases China's ability to keep the exchange rate stable and increases the confidence of the investors. In addition, in the second half of 1998, the international financial co-operation made the international financial markets head in a positive direction. This also helped the Chinese currency to keep its value.

Cutting interest rates made the loan rates drop by 5.17 percentage points since 1996. The one-year loan rate reduced from 12.06 per cent in January 1996 to 6.93 per cent in July 1997. If the interest cost is calculated according to the total net loan of 5,000 billion Yuan, the seven times slash of the interest rates will relieve industry from 240 billion Yuan interest payment.

This is very important, especially to the SOEs. Interest payment has been a large proportion of their financial liabilities and business costs. Decreasing the interest rate is very important to them in the situation of low profits and unemployment costs (factories have to pay minimum salaries to unemployed workers according to Chinese policy). In 1997 industry profits were slightly higher than in 1996, but increased profits had barely recovered from the interest rate relief. From January to August 1998 the SOEs suffered a net loss of profits. If there had been no interest rate cut, they would have suffered more.

In 1998 consumption increased steadily. In the second half of the year, it showed an increasing trend. The retail value increased by 6.8 per cent, after being adjusted for deflation. The retail value rose 9.4 per cent, and it was higher than the GDP growth rate. There are many factors affecting the increase of consumption demand, for example, the product structure may not be appropriate, or consumers may have low expectations for future income.

In 1999 the PBC enlarged the scope of the open market operations, increased the number of trade instruments, increased the number of traders trading treasury bills, increased trade, and improved clearing office operations in order to better implement open market operations.

Because the 1998 interest rate cut did not stimulate consumer demand to an expected level, in 1999 China utilized the following policies to stimulate consumption:

1. The PBC set new policies allowing all commercial banks to provide consumer loans. Mortgages and car loans increased in 1999. Commercial banks gave priority to borrowers who bought newly built apartments.
2. The PBC encouraged commercial banks to open new types of consumer loans, for example, loans for purchase of durable goods. In the meantime, the PBC amended the policies regarding debit card and personal chequing accounts in order to accommodate consumer loan development.
3. In 1999, for the first time, the PBC allowed the commercial banks to have freedom to choose either fixed rate loans or floating rate loans so that borrowers could avoid interest rate risks and to increase consumer requests for loans. The PBC also set the mortgage interest rates according to the term of mortgages.

In 2000 the money supply target was to increase the growth of GDP from 1999 and to control deflation. The policy was for stimulation of domestic demand and investment. The PBC increased the money supply and strengthened open market operations. The M2 increased by 12.3 per cent, M1 increased by 16 per cent and the M0 increased by 8.9 per cent. Consumer loans were newly introduced as banking tools to encourage borrowing. The commercial banks were allowed to expand their business. The mortgage and private consumption loans became major commercial bank loans. By issuing government bonds, the Ministry of Finance increased government investment in infrastructure, increased exports and stimulated economic growth.

The increase of the money supply in 2000 also encouraged an increase in investment and increased government purchasing of agricultural products. In China, the fixed capital investment and government purchasing of agricultural products are two ways to distribute the money supply. In 2000 the fixed capital investment increased by 9.3 per cent to 3.26 trillion Yuan RMB. Infrastructure investment increased by 6.1 per cent to 1.32 trillion Yuan RMB (H. Zhang, 2001).

In 2000 the Chinese currency maintained its value. As a result, the money supply remained stable. If inflation had occurred in 2000, the money supply would not have been stable and would have dramatically increased.

As a result of the monetary policy implementation in 2000, GDP growth rate was greater than that of 1999. This was the first sign of acceleration of growth since the 1997 Asian Financial Crisis. Deflation has been limited, and exports increased dramatically.

The PBC re-organization

Starting from 1998 the PBC restructured itself. It eliminated 31 province-level branches and 148 local branches. It set up 9 divisional branches throughout the country. This arrangement is similar to the Federal Reserve Bank system in the US. Three hundred and twenty-six central offices and 1827 county offices were established. They report to the divisional branches.

After the organizational reform, the new PBC came into operation on 1 January 1999. The PBC defined the functions of the four layers. The headquarters centralized the decision-making power for monetary policy. The divisional branches study the local financial situation and provide policy advice to the PBC headquarter. The branches and local offices do the work of financial supervision. They supervise all other financial institutions inside their territory, punish violations, analyse, prevent and eliminate financial risks. On service functions they are closer to financial institutions and enterprises. It is better to improve the service quality by using the new technology and equipment.

The new system of the PBC separates the responsibilities of the headquarters, branches, central offices and local offices while helping each other in the execution of monetary policy, financial supervision and on financial services. It is helpful for the PBC to set up a financial supervision network, increasing the ability to prevent and eliminate financial risks and making the financial market development smoother.

Stock market

Since its beginning in 1990, the stock market in Shanghai developed quickly. China later established another stock market in its southern city of Shenzhen. By 2000 there were more than 800 public traded companies and the total market cap is 2 trillion Yuan RMB, which was more than 20 per cent of the Chinese GDP.

The PRC amended its Securities Market Act in order to reduce financial risks such as stock manipulation, according to the *Taiwan Today News Network* on 29 December 1998. Fifteen articles of the Securities

Market Act of the PRC were amended and passed by the Sixth Meeting of the People's Congress Standing Committee on 29 December 1998 according to the Chinese official news agency – Xinhua Agency (Box 3.11).

Box 4.1 Securities Market Act

The Sixth Meeting of the People's Congress Standing Committee on 29 December 1998

The main parts of the amendment include: forbidding state-owned enterprises to invest in stocks, limiting the banking funds entering the stock market, in order to discipline the stock market, protect small investors, reinforce stock market management and protect the stock market from the attacks of international hedge funds.

The Articles 'forbidding state-owned enterprises to buy and sell stocks' and 'limiting banking funds flowing into stock markets' were added into the Act for the purpose of reducing the financial risks, because speculating stocks by state-owned enterprises and banks severely increases the risk exposure of state assets and manipulation of the markets.

The amended Act also includes 'The stock brokerage firms shall separate their own investment business from their brokerage business'. The reason for this is that 'Currently the brokerage firms heavily borrow money from their customers to speculate on the stock market' and there is significant potential risk.

Qiao Xiaoyang, vice-chairman of the Judiciary Committee of the People's Congress of China, said 'The Act Amendment defines that opening of stock trading accounts shall submit certified document of legal Chinese citizens or legal Chinese enterprises.' This is to protect the stock markets from attacks by international hedge funds.

The newly amended Securities Market Act also reinforces the following issues:

1. Initial public offering of stocks;
2. Monitoring the fund use of the collected money by issuing company stocks;
3. Forbidding day trading;
4. Supervision of the brokerage firms and clearing firms.

Source: Taiwan Today News Network, 29/12/1998.

The amendment focused on improving securities market regulations, reinforcing market discipline, and reducing financial risks.

4.4 Summary and discussion

The Chinese economy remained fairly stable throughout the Asian Financial Crisis between July 1997 and the spring of 1999. The consumer price index (CPI) in Table 4.3 (p. 91) showed stable prices in China, while in other Asian countries CPI increased significantly. Perhaps this was due, at least in part, to the sound conduct of monetary policy in China throughout this period. The stability oriented monetary policy and the active fiscal policy are two major points that support the Chinese economy. The monetary policy keeps interest rates low and increases commercial banking loans in co-ordination with the government bond issuing. At the same time, it keeps currency RMB exchange rate flat and maintains international trade balance.

The developing countries and developed countries might learn from China's successful banking reforms and ability to avoid financial crisis. Both the international banking and financial crises have the following characteristics (World Bank, 1997):

1. Recent banking crises have been frequent and severe.
2. The economies which were affected by the banking crises suffered severely.
3. The crisis cannot be attributed to a single factor.

Chinese financial reform and central banking reform can educate monetary authorities so that they can make better policy decisions in preventing the future financial crisis: 'He must have a long spoon that must eat with the devil' (Shakespeare, *The Comedy of Errors*, IV. iii. 65)

Arestis and Demetriades (1999) described some factors that contributed to the crisis, such as weaknesses in the legal framework governing the operation of financial markets, including bankruptcy laws and lack of transparency.[1]

The central bank has the responsibility to co-ordinate with the International Monetary Fund (IMF) to reinforce the financial restrictions. From the lessons of the Asian Financial Crisis, Katz (1999) describes following proposals for the IMF (eventually through the central banks) to consider (Box 4.2).

In the long run (more than five years), according to Dai (2002), China will implement tight monetary policy and prevent potential inflation.

Box 4.2   Proposals for the IMF by S.S. Katz

Enhanced transparency and accountability. Macroeconomic data as well as transactional information should in the future be based on uniform definitions and standards and should become rapidly and readily available to all public, private and international participants in international financial markets.

Stronger financial systems and financial market restructuring. The intent is to recognize that the liberalization of capital markets is an essential component of a well-functioning market-based economy, but that it should follow, not lead, the strengthening of financial sector institutions and the establishment of systems to record, monitor and, as appropriate, regulate capital transfers.

Control of foreign direct investment and regulation of speculative flows. This proposal would involve the imposition of reserve requirements on foreign borrowing or a negative interest rate or excise-type tax on short-term withdrawals, as well as the prioritizing of long-term capital investments so that resources would be directed to high priority investments, not to speculative or lower priority ventures.

Avoidance of the mismatch of borrowing and investment. This proposal would seek to avoid the use of short-term loans to finance long-term investments and to prevent short-term credits from being repeatedly rolled over as a substitute for long-term financing.

Source: S. S. Katz, 'The Asian Crisis, the IMF and the Critics', *Eastern Economic Journal*, 1999, vol. 25, no. 4.

But for a specific year, the money supply will be decided according to the international and domestic circumstances.

Notes

1. Arestis and Demetriades (1999) described some factors that contributed to the crises, such as weaknesses in the legal framework governing the operation of financial markets, including bankruptcy laws and the lack of transparency. One irony that Arestis found is that, before the 1997 crisis, the (South) East Asian economies were widely regarded as possessing a strong institutional

framework conducive to promoting economic growth. The 1997 crisis has also revealed the potentially destabilizing role that could be played by external financial liberalization, particularly the liberalization of short-term capital flows. *Ex post* one can once again blame it all on ineffective banking supervision, arguing that central banks should somehow be able to safeguard the banking system from known institutional weaknesses. However, this is clearly a tall order for any bank supervisor and is unlikely ever to be met in practice. Thus, to blame the banks is tantamount to maintaining a belief in a utopia, which would continue to result in expensive mistakes in the future.

A better approach, Arestis and Demetriades (1993) believe, is to drop utopian assumptions altogether and work within real-world constraints, rather than insist that the world should change to fit theoretical models, biases and preconceptions. In theoretical terms, this means developing models that take into account institutional weakness, information-related problems and so on. Meanwhile, in practical terms, a cautious approach should be pursued with respect to financial liberalization. Caution is particularly called for where institutions are weak, even if macroeconomic stabilization has been achieved. Thus, another prerequisite for financial liberalization must now be to strengthen the institutional framework, such as the legal system and government institutions, including the central bank.

5
The Impact of Membership of the World Trade Organization on the PBC's Monetary Policy

'I must go and meet with danger there,
Or it will seek me in another place
And find me worse provided.'

William Shakespeare, *Henry IV, Part 2*, II. iii. 48

5.1 Introduction

On 11 December 2001 China became a member of the World Trade Organization (WTO). China promised to cut import taxes within five years. On 1 July 2006 the automobile tax, for example, will decrease to 25 per cent from the current 30–80 per cent. In January 2002 the prices of imported products such as automobiles and agricultural products decreased dramatically.

Industrial products have an import tax of 11.6 per cent after joining WTO, whereas before China joined the WTO the import tax was 30–50 per cent. The automobile import tax decreased from 70 per cent to 43.8 per cent for cars with an engine capacity of less than three litres. The automobile import tax decreased from 80 per cent to 50.7 per cent for cars with an engine capacity of more than three litres. The import taxes for minivans with an engine capacity of less than three litres dropped from 45 per cent to 37.5 per cent. The taxes for minivans with an engine capacity of more than 3 litres dropped from 75 per cent to 47.5 per cent. For example, the retail price of a Lexus 430 dropped from 1.24 million Yuan RMB to 880 thousand Yuan RMB.

Agricultural products now have import taxes of 15.8 per cent, whereas before China joined the WTO the import tax was 30–60 per cent. Taking an example to show the impact, the price of imported grapes dropped from 460 Yuan RMB to 360 Yuan RMB per kilogram. Some consumer products such as big screen TVs had an import tax of 45 per cent prior to China's joining the WTO in 2001, and after 2001 the import tax was 36 per cent.

Because the prices of imported products are lower, there is an increase in competition between imported and domestic products. Because of this competition the prices of domestic products will fall in the future. Cutting the import tax results in the introduction of competition, and the imported products will force the domestic producers to make products of better quality. Production, marketing and sales will also improve.

Domestic agriculture will not disappear because of the presence of cheaper imported agricultural products in the market. The Chinese government still maintains an import quota on major agricultural products after 2001. This quota is much lower than that imposed before China joined the WTO.

Because the cost of imported raw materials decreased as a result of the import tax drop, domestic products may be produced more cheaply. Chinese people will enjoy lower prices of domestically produced products.

According to the 'Agreement on the Services of the World Trade Organization' (WTO), foreign banks will be allowed to compete in China in five years. During the next five years some foreign banks will be permitted to compete with domestic banks, and after five years unlimited competition will be permitted (Dai, 2002). Foreign banks will enjoy the same status as domestic banks. According to the 'Agreement on Trade-related Investment' of the WTO, China will gradually remove investment restrictions on foreign financial institutions during the next five years.

Monetary policy will also be affected. After joining the WTO, the dramatically increased international capital flow will dilute, sometimes may eliminate, the effect of the Chinese interest rate policy and foreign exchange policy. The foreign currency deposits will occupy a large proportion of the money supply. The trade balance will have more and more impact on the economy and the financial sector. Using money supply as a policy tool, its stability and controllability will become lower.

After China joined the WTO, foreign banks competed with local banks, but foreign commercial banks already conducted investment banking business. In order to create a competitive environment, some people support the idea that Chinese commercial banks should be allowed to conduct investment banking business. They say that a major benefit would be maximization of profits by utilizing the specialties of both kinds of banks. As we stated in Chapter 3, the separation of commercial banks and investment banks involves the questions of asymmetric information, adverse selection and other information economic theories. To apply these theories to the Chinese situation involves the theories of liberalization of financial markets stated first by the McKinnon–Shaw Model (McKinnon, 1973; Shaw, 1973), then by Arestis and Demetriades (1999).

5.2 Theories

Arestis and Demetriades' (1999) theory is very important in the modern version of financial liberalization theories (World Bank, 1989), including effective banking supervision and microeconomic stability. This version of financial liberalization is different from the McKinnon–Shaw theory that financial development affects the rate of GDP growth silently (endogenously) through the exogenous technical progress. The three assumptions (perfect information, profit-maximizing competitive behaviour by commercial banks, and institution-free analysis) of the McKinnon–Shaw theory are unlikely to be met in the real world. The reason is as follows.

The perfect information assumption could be harmed by the asymmetric information problem as stated in Chapter 2: in financial markets, one party often does not know enough about the other party to make accurate decisions.

Adverse selection is the problem created by asymmetric information before the transaction occurs. Adverse selection in financial markets occurs when the potential borrowers who make 'bad' credit risks are likely to promise the lenders a higher return than normal lenders could provide, thus they are likely to be chosen to get the loan. However, they have a 'bad' credit risk and will probably default on the loan. This is not what the lender (the bank) wants to see. Unfortunately, in the case of adverse selection this is what happens.

After the financial transaction occurs, a moral hazard problem can be created. Moral hazard in financial markets is the risk (hazard) that the borrower might engage in activities that are undesirable (immoral) from the lender's point of view because they make it less likely that the loan will be paid back.

All these information economic theories came after the early financial liberalization models such as the McKinnon–Shaw model. The McKinnon–Shaw model did not include the asymmetric information when they raised the three assumptions in designing the model. And it has defects in explaining the unsuccessful attempts of many developing countries liberalizing their financial systems in the 1970s and 1980s. For example, Venezuela and Uruguay in the early 1970s, Malaysia, Chile, Mexico, Brazil and Argentina in the mid- to late 1970s, and Indonesia, the Philippines, Turkey and Israel in the early 1980s, all implemented financial reforms. They all suffered 20 per cent interest rates, 'bad' debts, bank failures, bankruptcies, extreme asset volatility and the near-collapse of financial systems. Economists have tried to incorporate the asymmetric information problem into financial liberalization theories since then (Arestis and Dematriades, 1999). That is one of the reasons the new financial liberalization theories have developed differently.

A new model will be developed according to the asymmetric information theory: the lender should be able to distinguish the good borrowers from the bad, or those unlikely to repay the loan. The security market will then be able to move funds to the good firms that have the most productive investment opportunities.

To solve the adverse selection problem in financial markets is to eliminate asymmetric information by furnishing the lenders with full details about the individuals or firms seeking to finance their investment activities. One way to do this is to have private companies collect and produce information that distinguishes good from bad firms and then sell it to purchasers of their securities. In the United States, companies such as Standard and Poor's, and Moody's, gather information on firms' balance sheet positions and investment activities, publish these data and sell them to subscribers.

But people who do not subscribe to these services can take advantage of the information that other people have paid for. This is the free-rider problem. It prevents the private market from producing enough information to eliminate all the asymmetric information that leads to adverse selection. Now the government can help from this point. The government can supervise financial markets by encouraging firms to reveal honest information so that investors can determine how good or 'bad' the firms are. In the United States, the Securities and Exchange Commission (SEC) is the government agency that requires firms selling their securities in public markets to adhere to standard accounting principles and to disclose information about their sales, assets and earnings (Mishkin, 1998).

This theory was added to form the new model of financial liberalization. In the new model, many factors affect the outcome of financial liberalization: differential speeds of adjustment, competition of instruments (Sachs, 1988; see also p.128), macroeconomic instability and inadequate bank supervision.

Although government regulation lessens the adverse selection problem, it does not eliminate it. Even when firms provide information to the public about their sales, assets or earnings, they still have more information than investors: there is a lot more to know about a firm than statistics can provide. Furthermore, bad firms have an incentive to make themselves look like good firms because this would enable them to fetch higher prices for their securities. Bad firms will slant the information they are required to transmit to the public, thus making it harder for investors to sort out the good firms from the bad (Mishkin, 1998).

5.3 The decline of commercial banking business

From 1980 to the present, because of the steady growth of the stock markets and bond markets, people are likely to keep their life savings in the securities markets, especially when mutual funds significantly reduce the risks of investing in some specific companies. The commercial banks in Europe and the United States have been losing their customers. The dominant position of commercial banks has been changed.

As the Shanghai and Shenzhen stock markets develop, legislation has been reinforced. The mature stock markets will eliminate the hesitations of the Chinese on stock investments. As the stock markets grow, the Chinese commercial banks will see funds flowing out of savings accounts. In fact, the Chinese stock markets developed quickly since their beginning in 1990. By 2000 there were more than 800 public traded companies and the total market cap was 2 trillion Yuan RMB, which was more than 20 per cent of the Chinese GDP.

Another reason for the decline of commercial banking business is financial innovations which created investment opportunities with lower risk and higher return. These opportunities attracted people to move funds out of the commercial banks. For example, in the United States from the 1960s to the early 1980s financial innovations such as junk bonds, NOW ('negotiable order of withdrawal') accounts, and commercial papers cause the decline of the traditional business of the commercial banks. As the PRC allows foreign banks to conduct domestic currency business according to the 'Agreement on Trade-related Investment' of the World Trade Organization, the financial innovations from other countries will be accepted by Chinese investors. The Chinese commercial banking business might lose their customers in the future.

In China, introducing international financial operations and legislation caused the decline in cost advantages in acquiring funds (liabilities). The central bank controls interest rates and sets interest rate ceilings for commercial banks. The commercial banks cannot pay high interest on savings. During certain periods such as in mid-1993, the interest rates were even lower than the real rate of inflation. In China the high inflation rate in the mid-1980s, in 1988 and in 1992–3 led individual investors to remove funds from the commercial banks. The funds were invested in other places that provided higher yields. In Japan deregulation has provided many new financial instruments to the public, causing commercial banks a dramatic loss of deposits.

In China, commercial banks may lose loan business because their best corporate customers have had increasing access to foreign markets. The companies like Sohu.com and Sina.com raised funds in the NASDAQ ('National Association of Securities Dealers' Automated Quotation System') market in the United States. The increase of those activities in the future might cause the decline of commercial banking business in China.

Information technology has made it easier for companies to sell securities directly to the public, and commercial bank loans will have fewer borrowers. This also happened in the United States. Before 1970, non-financial commercial paper equalled less than 5 per cent of bank loans to commercial and industrial sectors, whereas the number has risen to over 20 per cent in 1996. In the United States, commercial paper is the major business of the finance companies. Before 1980 finance company loans to business equalled around 30 per cent of commercial and industrial bank loans; in 1996 they were over 60 per cent. In China, finance companies do not exist, but there are 70 financial corporations owned by state enterprises. Those enterprise investment funds will not be deposited in the commercial banks, but will remain with the enterprise. These funds will be managed by the subordinate financial corporations. At a certain level, the business of the financial corporations in China is similar to that of finance companies in the United States. The funds can be directed to other high-yield financial products.

In China, financial corporations underwrite securities directly or indirectly. For example, some of the securities are called 'collecting-money' ('Ji Zi' is the Chinese word) which is mainly oriented to employees inside the enterprises which own the financial corporations. The interest rates on these securities are much greater than those offered by the commercial banks. In the future, because people might not deposit funds in commercial banks, their business may decline. The central bank must consider this problem and try to prevent its occurrence.

Data from the United States show that the status of commercial banks as sources of funds for non-financial borrowers has declined dramatically. In 1974 commercial banks provided 35 per cent of these funds; by 1996 their market share decreased dramatically to 20 per cent. In addition, the commercial banks' share of total financial intermediary assets has fallen from approximately 40 per cent between 1960 and 1980 to less than 30 per cent by the end of 1996 (Mishkin, 1998).

5.4　Foreign competition and combination of commercial and investment banks

This chapter includes analyses of the problems faced by Chinese banks after foreign banks were allowed to compete with them under the 'Agreement on the Services of the World Trade Organization'. Several authors discussed these problems. Some of their proposals are examined in the following paragraphs.

S. Chen (2001) favours the combination of commercial and investment banks and thinks that 'a major benefit of allowing banks to invest in securities will be that commercial banks can get information about the financial status of public companies, this will decrease the asymmetric information and increase the quality of the loan'. This statement contradicts modern information economic theory.

The free-rider problem happens when private producers of information cannot obtain the full benefit of their information-producing services, thus less private information will be produced. As a result, there will be less information available to screen out good risks from bad risks. The bank can avoid the free-rider problem and profit by primarily making private loans rather than by purchasing securities that are traded in the open market. Because a private loan is not traded, other investors cannot watch what the bank is doing and bid up the loan's price to the point that the bank receives no compensation for the information it has produced, The bank's role as an intermediary that holds mostly non-traded loans is the key to its success in reducing asymmetric information in financial markets.

Mishkin (1998)'s analysis showed that financial intermediaries in general, and banks in particular, should play a greater role in moving funds to corporations than securities markets do because they hold a large fraction of non-traded loans.

The conclusion is that indirect finance is much more important than direct finance and banks are the most important source of external funds for financing businesses. In other words, commercial banks can gain nothing by sharing public information about enterprises in a perfect market.

Can a commercial-investment banking combination save the Chinese domestic banks from high competition from foreigners?

S. Chen (2001) further stated that:

> If investment banks cooperated with commercial banks, they can survive foreign banks' competition. The investment banks can use the commercial bank branches. They can benefit from the large customer base and clearing system of the commercial banks. The investment banks can increase their market share. Cooperating with commercial banks, the investment bank can use long-term loans, collateral associated loans and underwriting bonds to get funds easily.

In terms of increasing market share, however, it is possible that the competition is not only between domestic and foreign banks, but also among domestic investment banks. The policy change in China which allows merging of the commercial banks with investment banks will not give privileges to any particular bank in the competition. No bank can gain more market share than others.

It is of course possible that the competition is between domestic banks and foreign banks such as US banks. Recent legislation in the United States allowed US banks to function as both commercial and investment banks. The Chinese central bank does not permit the merging of investment banking business and commercial banking business. After China joined the WTO, the financial markets opened to foreign banks. The Chinese banks cannot compete because the separation of the two types of banks reduced their business opportunities. We agree that Chen's idea will help domestic banks in competition.

However, in China the financial system is not mature. The immediate easing of restrictions on the merging of the two types of banks may allow illegal operations in the new banks. For example, banks may use deposits to illegally speculate in the stock market or real estate market and suffer losses.

The mature international financial markets set strict rules for foreign banks. In their native countries, foreign banks have to obey rules which are more restrictive than those which Chinese banks must obey in China. Even though foreign banks have combined both commercial and investment banking, they will probably not act illegally because of their maturity and restrictive laws in their native countries.

The United States can be used as an example. The Federal Deposit Insurance Corporation (FDIC) Improvement Act of 1991 was passed to reduce the possibility of illegal operations by the banks.

In this Act the regulation involving deposit insurance was amended to reach this goal. A description of some parts of this regulation is as follows:

1. The FDIC is allowed to insure brokered deposits or accounts only if they are established under pension plans at well-capitalized banks.
2. The too-big-to-fail doctrine has been substantially limited: the FDIC must now close failed banks using the least costly method, thus making it far more likely that uninsured depositors will suffer losses.
3. To invoke the too-big-to-fail policy, a two-thirds majority of both the Board of Governors of the Federal Reserve System and the directors of the FDIC, as well as the approval of the secretary of the Treasury, would be required.
4. The FDIC Improvement Act requires that the Central bank share in the FDIC's losses.

5.5   Supervision of foreign banks and domestic banks

After joining the World Trade Organization, supervision of both foreign and domestic banks will increase the responsibility of the PBC.

Chartering and supervision of domestic banks

The PBC might learn from successful central banks in other countries which conduct sound monetary policies. In the future, more and more domestic banks will be chartered and enter the banking industry. Setting strict regulations for bank chartering is a good beginning of bank supervision.

PBC may learn from the United States in bank chartering. In the United States a commercial bank obtains a charter either from the Comptroller of the Currency (in the case of a national bank) or from a state banking authority (in case of a state bank). To obtain a charter, the people planning to organize the bank must submit an application that shows how they plan to operate the bank. In evaluating the application, the regulatory authority looks at whether the bank is likely to be sound by examining the quality of the bank's intended management, the likely earnings of the bank, and the amount of the bank's initial capital.

In China bank chartering mainly focuses on the shareholding banks. These banks are not state-owned and developed quickly. There were 110 shareholding commercial banks by 2001. The total assets were 2600 billion Yuan RMB, which was 19 per cent of the total commercial banking assets in China. Among them were nine cross country operated shareholding commercial banks with total assets of 1852.5 billion Yuan RMB and 99 local city commercial banks with total shareholding banks assets of $709.6 billion Yuan RMB (Deng, 2001). The shareholding banks could take risks in the stock markets if PBC supervision is not strict. The recent bankruptcy of the Guangdong International Trust and Investment Corporation (GITIC) is an extreme case for the PBC to pay attention to. The huge loss from GITIC bankruptcy would not have happened if it had not been chartered. Supervision begins with chartering banks.

Once a bank has been chartered, it needs to be tightly supervised. In the US, banks are required to file periodic (usually quarterly) call reports that reveal the bank's assets and liabilities, income and dividends, ownership, foreign exchange operations and other details. The bank is also subject to examination by the bank regulatory agencies to ascertain its financial condition at least once a year. National banks are examined by the Office of the Comptroller of the Currency, the state banks that are members of the Federal Reserve System are examined by the central bank, and non-members by the FDIC (Mishkin, 1998).

In China the difficult part of bank examination comes from city commercial banks and urban credit corporations. From 1978 to 2001, city commercial banks and urban credit corporations developed quickly. At the end of 1998 China had 88 city commercial banks, 3200 urban credit corporations, and 50,000 rural credit corporations. Their assets were 16.4 per cent of all commercial banking assets in China. They granted loans of 388.3 billion Yuan RMB in 2000 which represented an average annual increase of 56 per cent. Rural credit corporations also developed quickly. The annual increases of savings and loans between 1996 and 2000 were approximately 24 per cent. But some city commercial banks and rural credit corporations have problems in management, illegal lending and having a large amount of defaulted loans. It suggests that the chartering procedure should not only be strict at the beginning, but also should be followed up.

Supervision of foreign banks

PBC supervision of foreign banks will be difficult because the regulations are different between the PBC and foreign central banks. When foreign banks do business in China, how will the PBC supervise them? It is likely that the foreign banks will take more risks than they normally would in their own countries if the PBC does not exert adequate supervision.

There might be a conflict between the PBC and foreign central banks when bank regulation and supervision are involved. In our opinion, the PBC is correct in adopting the standards which have been accepted by the international financial community.

Since 1978 a large number of experiments have been performed by the PBC to improve the process of banking reform in China. Although these experiments have made significant achievements, the process is ongoing to improve the central banking system and monetary policy decision-making. The recent reforms also help the PBC to standardize regulations. Furthermore, they will help China to prepare for the future cooperation between the PBC and foreign central banks. The functions of the cooperation are supervision of foreign banks in China, establishment of rigid standards for the granting of loans by setting a risk-based capital requirement, prevention of financial crises by reducing risks taken by the banks, the establishment of reserve funds for 'bad' loans and coordination in bankruptcy cases to protect depositors.

Many financial fraud cases and financial crimes happened because of lack of supervision. The scandal of the Bank of Credit and Commerce International (BCCI) is an example of lack of supervision. It occurred in England in 1991 when it was found illegally moving funds to secret accounts in the Cayman Islands and then stealing the funds. BCCI had assets of $20 billion in its balance sheet, and owned branches in more than 70 countries. It was chartered in Luxembourg in 1972, and the chartering country Luxembourg should have supervised it. However, the Luxembourg monetary authority, Institut Monetaire Luxembourgeois, did not have ability to gather information on BCCI's operations and could not supervise it because it was headquartered in England and had international businesses in many countries. In 1987 the Institut Monetaire Luxembourgeois reached an agreement with seven other countries' regulators to oversee BCCI jointly, but even this larger group was unable to keep track of the bank's activities (Mishkin, 1998). Lessons should be learned from the BCCI scandal. The supervision of foreign banks is a difficult job and needs to be paid attention to after China's joining of the WTO.

5.6 Financial risks during financial liberalization

Introduction

Financial risks result in financial crises, which eventually cause recessions in the economy. China had ten historical financial crises between

1886 and 1948. Financial crises are unavoidable in other countries, too. In 1929 the financial crisis in the US caused the world economic recession which lasted some years, and was known in the US as the Great Depression. As a result of the depression the Glass-Steagell Act was passed in 1933. The British exchange rate crisis in the 1980s, the Mexican financial crisis in the 1990s, and the Asian Financial Crisis in 1997 occurred during the last century. The financial crisis in Argentina was rife as this book was written in the Spring of 2002.

After 1949 the financial system in China was based on the monobank system, the state centrally planned system, the credit plan and the cash plan. Most resources were owned by the state. The financial risks of the centrally planned economy are different from those of the free market economy. In the free market economy, the risks are created by the markets and resolved by the markets. The sequential reactions at the time of financial crisis are the failure of financial intermediaries, currency depreciation and bankruptcy. The ultimate responsibility must be borne by the investors.

However, China has a centrally planned economy, and the financial risks are different from those that exist in the free market economy. Even though some free market economic activity exists now, the Chinese economy is still largely affected by the centrally planned system. Should a financial crisis happen in China, the sequence would be commercial bank failure, the increase of the money supply by the central bank, and inflation. Various policy tools will be used to treat the different problems in the sequence. China should not necessarily use the methods of the West. Chinese financial risks might involve foreign exchange, the quality of new loans, and the supervision of SOEs and private/shareholding companies.

There are three financial risks in China–risks coming from international financial markets, interest rate risks and the default loan risks might be three of them.

Risks from international financial markets

The value of Chinese currency is allowed to float relative to the value of the US dollar. Thus risks in international financial markets will affect domestic financial markets. China has become a member of the international financial community. After it joined the World Trade Organization in December 2001, the influence of international markets became more pronounced in China. The capital flow from international sources has had a big impact on domestic financial markets. In addition, international financial risks cannot be eliminated by a single act of the central bank. Therefore, it is important to consider the influence of international financial crises on the economy of China, and try to determine ways to prevent their negative impact. There are several discussions involving the safety of the investment that the Chinese government has made in US treasury bills. Seventy per cent of the Chinese foreign exchange reserves, $144 billion, are invested in US treasury bills. In the event of an economic war or similar altercation between China and the United States, some people may be concerned that the US will not release the $144 billion. However, US companies have invested billions of dollars in the Chinese economy in the past two decades. The value of the American investments in many factories, plants, real estate projects and infrastructure is approximately equivalent to $144 billion. That eliminates the risks. Thus, some people think that there is no reason to be concerned. These people would be more concerned about the risk exposure of Hong Kong and Macao, both of which have the free foreign exchange markets and are vulnerable to international attacks. However, in addition to the cost of actual dollar, reputation cost should also be considered. Future investments will be discouraged.

Interest rate risks

The American savings and loan corporations crisis in the 1980s permitted the Chinese to prepare for future financial crises. From the 1960s to the early 1980s the American banking system incorporated several innovations such as junk bonds, NOW (Negotiable Order of Withdrawal) accounts and commercial papers. These innovations caused the decline of the traditional business of the commercial banks as stated earlier in Section 5.3. In the new wave of deregulation, the regulation and control were relaxed. The Depository Institutions Deregulation and Monetary Control Act of 1980, among other legislations, put an end to the Regulation Q and allowed savings and loan corporations to issue chequing accounts (NOW accounts). The Depository Institutions (Garn–St Germain) Act of 1982 authorized savings and loan corporations to offer money market funds and allowed them to make business and consumer loans. In 1983 several states relaxed their restrictions on direct investment in risky assets such as junk bonds, real estate ventures, and other high-risk low-quality business deals. The number of bank examiners was reduced and so too was the diligence of bank audit and examination. Many of these risky investments went sour, and this, coupled with increased fraud, embezzlement and mismanagement, led to a large number of bank failures in the United States in the 1980s.

The traditional savings and loan corporations were to acquire savings deposits and use these funds to make home mortgages. They 'were allowed to have up to 40 per cent of their assets in commercial real estate loans'. All those mortgages were traditionally made on a long-term fixed-rate basis, as long as 30 years. Savings deposits are payable on demand. So when short-term interest rates are too high, a bank would have to raise the rate it pays on savings deposits. But the savings and loan corporations were limited in their ability to raise savings deposit interest rates by Regulation Q. In addition, even if the savings and loan corporations could raise interest rates on savings deposits they would still be squeezed, because the long-term fixed rates received from mortgages were lower in many cases than the interest rates that they would have to pay to attract depositors. Depositors simply withdrew their savings and invested their money directly in higher yielding money market mutual funds.

China had a history of inflation in 1988 and 1993 when the government stimulated growth. In the future, the chance of bank failure caused by inflation as happened in the USA cannot be totally ruled out. At the same time financial innovation products are more and more popular for the commercial banks to use to boost profits while they increase the risks as well. So it is possible that a banking crisis could happen similar to that of the savings and loan corporations in the United States in the 1980s.

Default loan risks

In China, 80 per cent of the loans are provided by both state-owned and non-state-owned commercial banks, and the sources of the funds are savings deposits. Fifteen per cent of the loans are granted directly by enterprises. Five per cent are granted by foreign banks. Even though the loan ceiling policy was eliminated on 1 January 1998, there are still financial risks. The four state-owned commercial banks, which provide 75 per cent of commercial banking loans, are still controlled by the government. The state-owned commercial banks assist the Ministry of Finance. The government and the central bank will intervene to prevent the failure of the state-owned commercial banks. The four state-owned commercial banks will not go bankrupt because they are owned by the government. The financial risks for them are not significant.

The government safety net for depositors can avoid bank panics in China. It provides protection for depositors, and because of this protection depositors might be less reluctant to put funds in the banking system. This is like the Federal Deposit Insurance Corporation (FDIC) in the United States. Depositors are paid in full on the first $100,000 they have deposited in the bank if the bank fails. This number is being raised to $130,000. It has gone through both US House and Senate.

When Chinese people consider the bank panics of the late 1940s during the regime of Jiang Kai-shek, they can understand the importance of such a system. In 1948 the inflation rate was more than 10,000 per cent and at that time the value of money decreased dramatically daily.

Because of the immaturity of the Chinese stock market and the risk of investing in it, people prefer to deposit their money in the commercial banks. From 1990 to 1999 the growth rate of savings deposits was 28.6 per cent, which is much higher than the 16.2 per cent growth of salary increases. According to estimates from the Chinese Statistics Bureau, there are as much as 100 billion Yuan RMB deposits.

The quantity of this kind of savings deposit is becoming larger and larger. When the central bank increases the money supply, a large fraction of it is deposited in commercial banks. This money earns very little interest. The commercial banks have been reluctant to lend in recent years because they fear that the loans will not be repaid. (Large numbers of loans were not repaid in recent years.) These deposits cannot be invested in capital markets. It contributes little to the economy and is called idle cash.

Many people in China have little trust in the stock market, but have great faith in commercial banks. The researchers who prefer combining investment banks and commercial banks rely on that faith to support the new banks. The support might lead depositors to invest in the stock market.

This might be a quick way to attract investment because of the commercial banks' long history of credibility. However, if the new bank invests in the stock market and there are losses, this faith will be easily destroyed.

Deposits in the commercial banks are safe because the government guarantees their safety. The deposit insurance or the government safety net for deposits permitted moral hazard, the incentive of one party to a transaction to engage in activities detrimental to the other party. Moral hazard is an important concern in insurance arrangements in general because the existence of insurance provides increased incentives to the commercial banks for taking more risks that probably cause an insurance payoff.

Driven by the profit enthusiasm, commercial banks look for high-risk business. Adding fuel to the fire, financial innovation produced new financial instruments that widened the scope for risk taking.

The elimination of 'bad' loans will result from exercising more rigid standards in the granting of new loans. The new loans may become 'bad' loans. Controlling the quality of new loans will eventually cause the decrease in the number of 'bad' loans.

The coexistence of SOEs, shareholding companies and private companies increases the possibility of financial risk. The financial risks from the market-oriented private or shareholding companies can be handled by the monetary policies of the central bank. SOEs are subsidized by the government, benefit from low-interest loans, and are charged minimum prices for raw materials. Sales of their products are guaranteed. There is no incentive to improve the management or to innovate.

The majority of new loans will be of better quality if the credit histories of enterprises known by local offices of the central bank will advise the commercial banks. The central bank knows the reputations of enterprises which invest in real estate and stock markets, and it can communicate that information to commercial banks. Financial legislation will be passed to carefully define the relationship between foreign central bank control and PBC control of foreign financial institutions. The legislation will also define what funds from commercial banks can legally flow into the stock market. For example, if an enterprise gets a loan from a commercial bank, then uses the loan for production, and goes on to sell the product, can the enterprise use the proceeds to invest into the stock market? Is this investment illegal from the supervision point of view?

The four state-owned commercial banks grant 75 per cent of all commercial banking loans. The default risk is higher than that of non-state-owned banks because state-owned commercial banks grant more loans. The state-owned commercial banks are not as careful as non-state-owned commercial banks in granting loans because they are backed by the government, and they cannot go bankrupt. The default loans cannot cause bankruptcy of the state-owned commercial banks.

The stock market risk is different. By the year 2000 there were more than 800 companies listed on the stock markets. They raised US$32 billion by issuing stocks. Total market value equals US$240 billion, roughly 23 per cent of the Chinese GDP. The regulations involving the stock markets are still being changed and are not complete. Because of the incomplete regulation, the stock market risk is the biggest risk in the Chinese financial markets. In the Chinese stock market, there are two types of shares: A-shares, open to Chinese citizens, and B-shares, open to foreigners. Since June 2001, B-shares have been open to Chinese citizens, too. The mixture of foreign currency and local currency increases the chances of stock manipulation and speculation by a foreign hedge fund, which in fund size can be compared to a 'blue whale' versus the 'small fish' of the domestic companies. Even worse, if the stock market crashed, the potential for destruction of the economy is much greater than that of the default loan risks.

'Bad' loans issue

Four commercial banks belong to the state, and the government will insure the deposits in these banks. Because of this government safety net, the banks can make questionable investments with the intent of making higher profits. For example, in the inflation period in 1993, banks granted loans to companies that invested in the real estate and security markets. When the real estate markets crashed in 1993, many of the loans could not be repaid.

Overdue loans, which are not repaid during a two-year period, and default loans that are not repaid, are 'bad' loans in China. In some instances loans that are repaid during a two-year period are considered loans that are not repaid. By 1998 as much as 2.9 per cent of the loans granted by commercial banks were not repaid, and as a result the commercial banks have lost 100 billion Yuan RMB (Gao, 2001).

Based on several other studies, the 'bad' loans in China come from five sources:

1. The transition of the centrally planned system to the market economy caused loans left from the old economic system to remain unpaid. Agricultural reform eliminated the collective units in the rural areas. The loans granted to the collectives could not be repaid. During industrial reform in the 1980s, the government stopped guaranteeing the sales of products from some SOEs. These enterprises could not repay the loans from the commercial banks because they could not sell their products.
2. When the economic structure changed, the economic sectors such as the export industry and consumer product manufacturing were losing money because of the Asian Financial Crisis in South East Asia in 1997 and deflation in China in 1998. Some loans granted to businesses in these sectors were not repaid.
3. The PBC regulations of bank loans were inadequate, and some overdue loans could not be repaid.
4. Government mismanagement of resource allocation and its mistakes in enterprise production plans caused loss of profit. Some loans were not repaid.
5. Borrowers' mismanagement causes losses in the operations and the loans cannot be repaid.

'Bad' loans can cause inflation. Default loans will limit the commercial banks' ability to pay depositors. Lack of payment by the commercial banks will require them to apply to the PBC for discount loans. The large numbers of discount loans and inadequate regulation of the process of granting these loans might lead to inflation. The default loans were then changed to default discount loans. The PBC and Ministry of Finance have less funds in the discount window than usual. Insufficient discount funds cause a fiscal deficit, and finally defeat effective monetary policy that aims to fight inflation, and as a result inflation cannot be controlled. Now 'bad' loans are managed by the newly established asset management corporations, which are independent from the banks, the 'bad' loans are still losses to PBC. The balance sheet of the PBC piles up many 'bad' loans. The PBC has to increase the money supply to cover losses from 'bad' loans. The increase of the money supply for covering the 'bad' loans distorts the estimate of the money supply as a monetary policy tool. It will be difficult for the PBC to conduct the monetary policy with unreliable estimation. Ineffective monetary policy cannot control inflation.

Since 1998 the PBC has been using stabilization-oriented monetary policy to increase the money supply. The PBC cut the interest rates four times and cut the reserve ratio. The PBC improved the open market operation, and told the commercial banks to restructure loans. Even good monetary policy is ineffective when the amount of money involved in 'bad' loans is very large. For example, the total loan amount decreased significantly since 1997 even though the monetary policy was supposed to stimulate the issue of new loans. The growth rate for the new loans was 15.5 per cent, 12.4 per cent and 13.4 per cent for the years 1998, 1999 and 2000.

'Bad' loans can cause the loss of the monetary policy target. The final target of monetary policy is to maintain currency value and to stimulate GDP growth. In order to reach the target, monetary policy tools such as interest rate or money supply M2 are used. We can conclude from Table 5.1 that the money supply in the PRC grew at a diminished rate. It fell 13 per cent from 1996 to 2000 with an annual rate decrease of 3.25 per cent.

Table 5.1 The M2 growth rate, 1996–2000 (%)

	1996	1997	1998	1999	2000
M2 growth	25.3	17.3	15.3	14.7	12.3

Source: People's Bank of China, *ACFB: Almanac of China's Finance and Banking*, 1997–2001.

The explanation for the diminished growth rate of the M2 follows. As a monetary policy tool, the money supply is unstable in the short term because Chinese economic reform has a short history of 20 years. China has limited experience in monetary policy implementation. Ultimately M2 growth will reach its long-term equilibrium and will remain stable. From 1988 to 1994 the high growth rate permitted the granting of a large number of loans. Ultimately many of these loans became 'bad' loans. These loans resulted in major losses to the banks. Then banks have less money to lend, and are more cautious when granting new loans and often refuse new loans. Since fewer new loans are granted, the money supply has limited effects and cannot stimulate economic growth through the increase of new loans. In addition, the 'bad' loans will decrease the capacity of commercial banks to grant loans. Because enterprises cannot obtain enough capital, productivity and revenue drop. The decrease in revenue results in a higher unemployment rate. High unemployment reduces consumer demand and causes economic growth to slow.

'Bad' loans affect the base money supply. In order to write off default loans, the PBC has to increase the money supply. The base money will increase as well. Then the PBC has to sell treasury bills through open market operations to reduce the circulated money. For example, in 2000, discount loans of 286 billion Yuan RMB were granted, including 174.5 billion Yuan RMB loans to the four newly formed asset management corporations which will be described in the next section. To prevent the excess cash flow to the banks, the PBC increased open market operations since August 2000 by selling treasury bills in order to counterbalance the extra cash flow (Gao, 2001).

Solution of the 'bad' loan problem

In order to prevent future inflation caused by 'bad' loans in China, it is very important to minimize the losses from 'bad' loans. The central bank created four asset management corporations to manage 'bad' loans. Improvement of the commercial banks' liability structure, concentration on the management of 'bad' loans, the separation of old and new loans, and the adoption of more rigid standards for the granting of new loans are the purposes of the corporations.

Four asset management corporations – Xinda, Huarong, Great Wall and Eastern Asset Management Corporations – were established in 1999 after the approval of the State Council. They help financial firms to solve default loan problems and rejoin the commercial loan markets. They effectively eliminate financial risks and maintain financial stability. The 'good' and 'bad' loans were separated. If the 'bad' loan problem cannot be resolved effectively, the borrowers may be granted new loans to repay 'bad' loans. The new loans become 'bad' loans if they are not repaid. It is better if the banks can create the system which prevents enterprises from receiving new loans in order to repay 'bad' loans. In addition, it is important that loans granted by administration orders should not be tolerated. It also helps to increase the information network of getting borrowers' credit histories, increasing legislation, improving the responsibility of the loan makers, and increasing the risk management and crisis prevention alert system.

By 2001 'bad' loans of 1.39 trillion Yuan RMB were transferred to the four asset management corporations from the commercial banks. These loans included 'debt-switch-to-stock' loans of 410 billion Yuan RMB, overdue loans of 810 billion Yuan RMB and default loans of 170 billion Yuan RMB. These are the costs of the Chinese reforms and the transition to the market economy. Other countries also had this problem before, such as the home loan mortgage association crisis in the Britain in 1970s, the financial crisis in Japan in 1990s and the savings and loan corporations' crisis in 1980s in the United States.

In order to minimize losses from 'bad' loans, the market rule has to be reinforced. Some 'bad' loans can be converted from loans to stock shares. Eventually the shares can be sold by a stock buy-back plan, a stock option transfer or an initial public offering in order to return the principal to lenders. The value of overdue loans decreases with time, and authorities can restructure the assets and debts of the enterprises which received them. The enterprises will improve their management and become profitable so that they can repay the loans.

The 'bad' loans can also be sold at auction to foreign investors in order to change the overdue loans to active loans. In addition, the enterprises holding 'bad' loans can be restructured. After restructuring, the loans will be sold in the market. The auctioning or leasing of collateral is another way to minimize losses due to 'bad' loans. The proceeds from the auction or lease are paid to the commercial banks. For the default loans, an auction can get as much money back as possible.

In order to deal with the loss from the 'bad' loans, it shall be broken into a 15-year long-term loan. Thus the annual loss from the loan cannot cause inflation.

Central bank supervision is necessary to prevent questionable practices by banks. In 2001 in his report to the People's Congress on the Tenth Five-Year Plan, Premier Zhu Rongji emphasized the importance of financial supervision. He said that improving financial supervision would be important in Chinese future development. Financial supervision would be composed of the following points:

1. The PBC will supervise the commercial banks' overdue and defaulted loans;
2. Commercial banks should keep 8 per cent of the capital requirements which is the international standard;
3. The PBC will set up a cautious accounting system which will help supplement capital requirements, write off default loans and calculate the out-of-balance business. The commercial banks can have rights to write off 'bad' loans quickly.
4. The PBC will publish the definitions of the five categories of loans (Box 5.1). The possibility of the repayment of loans will be utilized to assess the market price of loans.
5. As the financial supervising organization, PBC will establish the supervision information system.
6. The information release of both the PBC and the commercial banks will be emphasized. The banks will become more transparent to the public so the market can have a binding force on the banks.

The reserve requirements for 'bad' loans

Before 1998 all the 'bad' loans had to be reported to the State Council. After approval by the State Council, the 'bad' loans can be written off by using the fund for regular loans. In 1998 MOF of China published 'The Temporary Stipulation on the Establishment of a Commercial Bank Fund for Default Loans' to allow the commercial banks to establish a special fund for the writing off of 'bad' loans left from previous years. Both the 'Accounting Rules for the Financial and Insurance Industries', and the 'Amendment of the Calculation of the Mature Time and Withdrawing the Reserve Fund for Default Loans', were published in 1998 by the MOF. They stipulated that 1 per cent of the total loans at the year end should be established as a 'bad' loan reserve fund.

There are some major defects involving the current 'bad' loan reserve fund in China. The ratio of the 'bad' loan reserve (it is manually defined by the PBC as a proportion of the total loans which must be put aside as cash against 'bad' loans) was very low before 1998. For example, the reserve ratio for 'bad' loans was 0.1 per cent for industry, commerce and construction and 0.15 per cent for the import–export sector before 1992. From 1992 to 1993 it was 0.5 per cent. Since 1993 it has risen to 0.6 per cent and has increased by an annual rate of 0.1 per cent. Compared with

Citigroup in the United States, which has a 2.74 per cent reserve fund for 'bad' loans (Li *et al.*, 2001), the Chinese ratio is very low.

Another defect is that the ratio is not linked to the management quality of the commercial banks. In China, all the banks have the same 1 per cent ratio regardless of quality of loans in different banks.

The four asset management corporations benefit from the experiences of similar organizations in other countries. Their major functions are buying, operating and managing the 'bad' assets obtained from commercial banks. In addition, the PBC entrusts the financial asset management corporations with careful management of small-sized financial institutions. They prepare the conditions to reactivate and reorganize the 'bad' loans, and set up restricted responsibility. The asset management corporations are built by the central bank. They get government funds and implement profit-oriented management. They set up the effective stimulation and self-restriction mechanisms, clearing reporting systems and highly transparent information release mechanisms. They do not belong to the commercial banks. They receive supervision from the central bank, and report to the PBC and the State Council periodically. According to periodic reports, the PBC sets risk-based banking capital requirements, as the United States does.

In the United States, there are three types of risk-based banking capital requirements. The first is based on the leverage ratio, the amount of capital divided by the bank's total assets. A bank's leverage ratio must exceed 5 per cent in order to be classified as well capitalized.

In order to solve the problem caused by banks' holding of risky assets and the increase in off-balance-sheet activities, such as fee-based letters of credit and loan commitments, a second type of risk-based capital requirement was introduced in December 1992. The banks must meet, along with the leverage ratio capital requirement, minimum capital standards linked to off-balance-sheet activities such as interest-rate swaps and trading positions in futures and options (Mishkin, 1998).

In 1996 the Federal Reserve in the United States announced a third type of capital requirement to take effect by January 1998. The Federal Reserve require banks to use their own internal models to calculate how much they could lose over a ten-day period and then set aside additional capital equal to three times that amount.

Experiences in the United States provide examples for the Chinese central bankers. In China, the PBC requires commercial banks to hold risk-based capital, based on the document 'Categorization of Loans Based on Risk' published by PBC in 1998 (Box 5.1).

Box 5.1 'Categorization of loans based on risk'
(issued by PBC in 1998)

1. Normal loans shall have risk-based capital requirement of 5 per cent;
2. First-level small risk loans shall have risk-based capital requirement of 5 per cent;
3. Second-level high risk loans shall have risk-based capital requirement of 20 per cent;
4. Loans likely to be defaulted on shall have a risk-based capital requirement of 50 per cent;
5. Default loans shall have a risk-based capital requirement of 100 per cent.

Examination of banks for risk-based capital requirements

The Chinese central bank learns how to do bank examination from the experiences of US central bankers. According to US banking supervision, the so-called on-site bank examinations, which allow regulators to monitor whether the bank is complying with capital requirements and restrictions on asset holdings, function to limit the lending risks. It is composed of five areas, capital adequacy, asset quality, management, earnings and liquidity. If the bank cannot get proper rating on those five areas, the bank examiners will take actions called cease and desist orders to change the bank's conduct or close a bank (Mishkin, 1998).

The bank examiners in the US make unannounced visits to the bank, and study a bank's books to see whether it is complying with the rules and regulations that apply to its holdings of assets. If a bank is holding securities or loans that are too risky, the bank examiner can force the bank to get rid of them. If a bank examiner decides that a loan is unlikely to be repaid, the examiner can force the bank to write off the loan. If the examiner feels that the bank does not have sufficient capital or has engaged in dishonest practices, it can be declared a problem bank and will be subject to more frequent examinations (Mishkin, 1998).

Based on these experiences in the US, Li *et al.* (2001) raised the following proposal to prevent 'bad' loans (Box 5.2).

Box 5.2 Proposal for improving the reserve requirement for the 'bad' loan system

The commercial banks shall be allowed to reserve two types of 'bad' loan reserve fund. One is the 1 per cent regular reserve fund. It writes off the default loans. The other type is the categorization of loans according to the risk. The ratio will depend on the risk. The PBC already has the 'Directions for the Categorization of Loans According to Risk'. But to adopt the directive immediately may present some difficulties. A two-step method shall be considered:

1. The first step will be adopted in 2002. The rate will differ according to how long overdue it is. For example, if the overdue time is less than 90 days, the ratio is 2 per cent; from 91 days to 365 days, the ratio is 10 per cent; from one to two years, 20 per cent; from two to four years 50 per cent; over four years overdue, 100 per cent.
2. The second step will start from 2003. The risk-based capital requirement will depend on the 'Categorization of Loans According to Risk'.
3. The capital requirement shall cover more loans including collateral-based loans and inter-bank lendings. In the meantime, the regulations shall be eased in order to allow more loans to be treated as default loans.
4. The PBC shall grant commercial banks rights to define default loans and write off default loans instead of reporting to the PBC for approval before writing them off. The MOF, taxation authorities and the State Council shall not require banks to write off or not to write off default loans. The write off of default loans shall be treated as a business secret. It should not be made public.
5. Clarify the responsibilities of each party. The PBC shall set up the capital requirement including the definition of the default loan and the minimum capital requirement, and conduct the bank examination. The MOF and the Taxation Department shall decide whether the funds for writing off default loans will be exempt from tax.

Source: Li *et al.* 2001.

More careful supervision by the central bank and better management by commercial banks have resulted in new loans of better quality. They are granted by state-owned commercial banks. Annual deposits in the four state-owned commercial banks increased by 700–800 billion Yuan RMB in 2000. The government deficit was 1.7 per cent of GDP, and the net annual increase of treasury bills was 10 per cent of GDP. There is enough money to deal with the 'bad' loans, and reforms in commercial banking and SOEs have resulted in fewer of them.

Bankruptcy issue

A significant amount of 'bad' loans could cause bank failure. Should bank failure happen, the financial institutions have the following ways to leave the financial market when their liabilities are greater than their assets. The banks can close themselves, they can decide to merge with another financial institution, or they can go bankrupt. Most companies do not want to leave the financial markets voluntarily.

If the financial institutions do not want to leave, the PBC has to rescue them by exchanging new funds for bank shares, forcing a merger with another financial institution, converting bonds to stocks, or assuming the management of the institution. In China all of the above ways have been used. For example, in September 1996 the Guangdong Development Bank bought the Chinese Bank of Trust and Investment. In October 1996 the PBC reorganized the Guang Da International Trust and Investment Corporation by converting its debt to stocks. In September 1995 the PBC took over the Chinese Bank of Trust and Investment.

When a financial institution violates the financial regulations, the PBC will close it according to law. When a financial institution's liabilities are greater than assets and the institution cannot repay the overdue debts, the PBC will also close it. After closing it, the PBC will organize an accounting group to calculate the assets. If necessary, the PBC will appoint an organization to manage the closed financial institution. After calculation of the assets, the major debtors and investors will arrange a meeting to discuss the debt reorganization and the formation of a new company. The newly formed company will be examined by the PBC and is given the new licence to do business after it passes inspection. If the reorganization fails and the parties do not agree with the PBC's plan on the calculation of the assets, the financial institution applies to the local court for bankruptcy. Then the bankruptcy is controlled by the courts. For example, on 6 October 1998 the PBC decided to close the Guangdong International Trust and Investment Corporation (GITIC). On 11 January 1999 the Guangdong International Trust and Investment Corporation (GITIC) applied for bankruptcy. For calculating the assets of GITIC, the PBC organized an accounting group and a management group with 150 professionals involved. The PBC hired Bimaweihua Accounting Office as the accounting consultant and hired Junxin Law Office as the legal consultant. They identified 27,937 individual debtors with a total debt of 0.78 billion, 571 organization debtors with a total debt of 36.75 billion Yuan RMB. The total liability for GITIC was 36.165 billion RMB. The total assets were 21.471 billion Yuan RMB. There was a shortage of 14.694 billion Yuan RMB. Total liability was less than assets, and the GITIC was announced bankrupt.

5.7 Chinese monetary policy: some topics

'Optimum order' theory in the decentralization of financial systems

Sachs (1988) described the concept 'competition of instruments' in his book *Developing Country Debt and Economic Performance*. The financial tools liberalized by the monetary authorities could have a conflict of interest, could have conflicting effects in operation and could thus offset each other. For example, if a system with government intervention opens the financial market to foreign banks and starts to decentralize the domestic financial markets simultaneously, both will compete with each other. Foreign banks will dominate the market due to the lack of experience of domestic banks. The economy will become more and more dependent on foreign investments and foreign 'instruments'. Eventually it will be vulnerable to any fluctuations of the international financial environment. To make things even worse, if the developing country is small, such as Thailand, the total central banking reserve cannot match the figure managed by a US mutual fund company or some hedge fund companies, and manipulation of markets cannot be avoided in the foreign exchange market where the local currency is pegged to the US dollar or in the stock market. Driven by profit-taking greed, foreign companies such as hedge funds are likely to attack the immature financial markets in developing countries, precipitating a financial crisis. Thus simultaneous opening of financial markets to foreigners and decentralizing them will not work.

Sequencing becomes important in liberalizing financial markets. For example, the liberalization of the domestic market should happen before opening doors to foreign markets. In practice, Gautier (1990) analysed Indonesian financial liberalization and found that the economy should be stable and banking supervision should be in place. Only after those two conditions are fulfilled, can financial liberalization have the chance to do its job. This sequence is the key. Indonesia's lessons were that both of the two prerequisite conditions were not met. This paper strongly supported the 'sequence' theory of the financial liberalization.

Recently, McKinnon (1993) came up with the concept of 'the optimum order of economic liberalization' to discuss how fiscal, monetary, and foreign exchange policies are sequenced is of critical importance. 'Government cannot, and perhaps should not, undertake all liberalizing measures simultaneously. Instead, there is an "optimal" order of economic liberalization, which may vary for different liberalizing economies depending on their initial conditions.' Some other papers also support a gradual and properly sequenced financial liberalization (Dickie, 1997).

Is there a general sequence for all the developing countries undergoing financial liberalization? The answer would be 'no'. As with the question 'Is there a universal defect shared by all Asian countries which caused the crises in 1997?', a positive answer cannot be given. The development of monetary policies, fiscal policies and foreign exchange policies for different countries depends on the characteristics of the economy, financial supervision, the market and political stabilization. Even though there is no uniform magic sequence for all the countries undertaking financial liberalization, proper order of development is still needed when the economic structure is changing in financial markets, because financial markets cannot be left to manage themselves during structural change (Johnston, 1990).

The stop–go pattern of Chinese economic and monetary policy

Table 5.2 is the money velocity and financial depth measurement for China (1979–99). Chapter 2 (p. 37) introduced other researchers' analyses of the money velocity between 1979 and 1993. They found that the policy changes affected the value of M1/GDP which is the financial depth of the Chinese economy. From 1979 to 1993, the Chinese economy suffered from persistent stop–go cycles in this reform period. I collected new data from 1993 to 1999 and used these data to examine the Chinese central banking policy changes and the impact on the economy. M1 is the currency in circulation plus demand deposits. M2 is M1 plus time deposits. Quasi-money is the difference between M2 and M1. M1/GDP is the financial depth of the Chinese economy and quasi-money/GDP is the non-monetary depth of the economy.

Table 5.2 The money velocity and financial deepening measurement for the PRC, 1979–99

Year	GDP	CPI	M1	Quasi-money	M2	M1/ GDP	Quasi-money/GDP	M2/GDP	Velocity = GDP/M2
1979	398.9	102.0	92.2	40.6	132.8	0.231	0.102	0.333	3.004
1980	446.7	106.0	114.9	52.2	167.1	0.257	0.117	0.374	2.673
1981	477.0	102.4	134.5	63.3	197.8	0.282	0.133	0.415	2.412
1982	518.9	101.9	148.8	77.8	226.6	0.287	0.150	0.437	2.290
1983	579.5	101.5	174.9	96.4	271.3	0.302	0.166	0.468	2.136
1984	693.8	102.8	244.9	115.0	359.9	0.353	0.166	0.519	1.928
1985	855.0	108.8	301.7	185.8	487.5	0.353	0.217	0.570	1.754
1986	970.0	106.0	385.9	249.0	634.9	0.399	0.257	0.655	1.528
1987	1133.0	107.3	457.4	338.3	795.7	0.404	0.299	0.702	1.424
1988	1404.0	118.5	548.7	411.5	960.2	0.391	0.293	0.684	1.462
1989	1598.6	117.8	583.4	555.9	1139.3	0.365	0.348	0.713	1.403
1990	1774.0	102.1	701.0	767.2	1468.2	0.395	0.432	0.828	1.208
1991	1976.0	102.9	898.8	961.1	1859.9	0.455	0.486	0.941	1.062
1992	2665.1	105.4	1282.0	1497.8	2779.7	0.481	0.562	1.043	0.959
1993	3447.7	113.2	1565.0	1892.8	3458.0	0.454	0.549	1.003	0.997
1994	4675.9	121.7	2054.0	2628.4	4682.4	0.439	0.562	1.001	0.999
1995	5847.8	114.8	2397.0	3426.0	5823.0	0.409	0.586	0.996	1.004
1996	6788.5	106.1	2851.0	4758.5	7609.5	0.420	0.701	1.121	0.892
1997	7446.3	100.8	3483.0	5616.9	9099.5	0.466	0.751	1.217	0.822
1998	7834.5	100.2	3895.4	6500.0	10449.9	0.464	0.815	1.279	0.782
1999	8191.1	100.2	4583.7	7406.1	11989.8	0.559	0.904	1.464	0.683

Notes: GDP: Gross domestic product (billion Yuan; 1 US dollar is equal to 8.31 Yuan in December 1999),CPI: Consumer price index calculated by chain-weight method using each previous year data as 100.
M1 is the currency in circulation plus demand deposit of banks. M2 is M1 plus time deposits from industries and agriculture, savings deposits and other deposits. Quasi-money is the difference between M2 and M1.
Source: People's Bank of China, Almanac of China's Finance and Banking, various issues.

Table 5.2 shows that in 1993 M1/GDP dropped to 0.454. M1 in 1993 increased only 22 per cent which is smaller than the previous annual increase of 42 per cent in 1992. When compared with GDP growth, the money supply (which is equivalent to credit expansion) decreased. This is because of the following policy adjustment. In 1992 Deng Xiao-ping's tour to Shenzhen city stimulated investment and development. Primier Li Peng announced the revision of the GDP growth target to 8–9 per cent from the original 6 per cent in the annual economic speech at the First Plenary Session of the Eighth National People's Congress on 15 March 1993. The administrative policy adjustment created an investment fever in 1992–3. The Chinese economy was overheated. Business demand for credit soared. From the second quarter of 1992 to the second quarter of 1993, huge sums were invested in the real estate market in the coastal areas. The financial institutions treated the inter-bank lending market as an easy and low-cost place to raise funds. Because of the lack of central bank control, some of the financial institutions borrowed heavily from the inter-bank lending market to invest in long-term projects with higher risks such as real estate in order to realize high profits. This caused the money velocity, as shown in Table 5.2, to decrease from 1.062 in 1991 to 0.959 in 1992 and 0.997 in 1993. Since velocity is GDP/M2, the decrease is because of either GDP decrease or the money supply (M2) increase. In addition, the CPI increased to 13 per cent in 1993 from 5 per cent in the previous year. These changes reflected the impact of policy on the economic growth.

In Table 5.2 this trend can be seen between 1994 and 1995, as the M1/GDP decreased to 0.439 in 1994, and 0.409 in 1995. The CPI increased to 21 per cent in 1994. This suggested that the 1993 reform did not achieve the expected result. Further policy adjustment was needed.

The 1995 reform package came with the 18 March legislation which defined the responsibilities of the central bank. It also separated commercial banking from investment banking business. The commercial banks are not permitted to invest in real estate that is not occupied by the commercial bank itself. The 10 May legislation prohibits commercial banks from investing in non-bank financial institutions and industrial enterprises. The legislation stipulates that commercial banks are prohibited from attracting savings deposits by manipulating interest rates. In addition, commercial banks are required to hold cash reserves with the PBC. These policy adjustments increased the expansion of M1 by 19 per cent in 1996, which was much more than the 16 per cent in 1995. The financial depth (M1/GDP) started to increase. The CPI dropped to 6 per cent in 1996, when compared with 14 per cent in 1995.

From 1997 to 1998, the CPI was decreasing, which was a positive indicator, while the financial depth (M1/GDP) decreased abnormally. This is because the high discount rate prevented banks from granting new loans and because the number of default loans increased. Banks were reluctant to grant new loans. Enterprises, especially small enterprises, could not get loans for the increase of production.

The above analyses show that the long-existing 'stop–go' cycle still existed during the recent reforms of the late 1990s. Is it a coincidence or a 'Chinese pattern'? How will it affect policy-making in the future? Will the authorities consider the 'stop–go' cycle while making decisions? Further studies are needed.

Figure 5.3 shows that the annual net loan increase is roughly equal to the net increase in M2 in 1988–90. After 1991 the net increase in M2 is greater than the net increase of loans. Before 1 January 1998 the PRC still used loan ceilings to control domestic demand. The credit plan and cash plan was used by the PBC to control credit. The initial design of control of credit was based on allocation of difference between deposits and loans granted. The branches which have surplus deposits have to submit the surplus deposits to PBC. The central bank (PBC) controls the money supply by control of loans granted by the commercial banks. In Figure 5.3 the difference between the net loan increase and the net money supply (M2) increase shows that PBC's monetary policy is buffered and it is made less effective. Even when PBC increases money

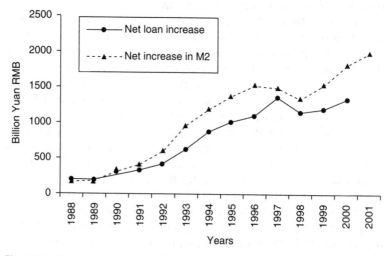

Figure 5.1 Net loan increase and M2
Source: People's Bank of China, *ACFB*, 1997–2001.

supply by setting a high loan ceiling, commercial banks are reluctant to grant new loans because of fear of default. The individuals and households are hesitant to invest in the stock markets because Chinese stock markets are not completely mature. The increased money supply cannot be fully injected into enterprises. The effect of the expansion-oriented monetary policy will be discounted. Thus the difference between M2 increase and loan increase is becoming greater.

5.8   The possibility of float of interest rates in the PRC

Introduction

The money market grows rapidly in China. The money market growth created the conditions for China to remove interest rate restrictions. Interest rates were dictated by the PBC and sometimes they do not reflect equilibrium values. China joined the WTO on 11 December 2001. The Chinese financial market will be open to foreign financial institutions in five years. It usually takes three years to finish floating the interest rates in a country. If the PRC begins to reform the interest rate system, there will be two years left for the domestic financial institutions to prepare for competition with foreign financial institutions.

Theory

There are some theories which involve discussion of letting markets decide interest rates. If China decides to float commercial loan interest rates suddenly, the change might cause chaos which would be similar to that of 1993. The PRC is a big country and economic policy should emphasize stabilization first (International Conference on Monetary Policy, 2001). Experience from other countries shows that gradual change in interest rates might be an alternative method to establish market equilibrium. Korea's interest rate floating is an example of gradual reform. It also took a long time to establish a floating interest rate system in the US and Japan.

In the PRC the commercial banks have granted 80 per cent of all loans annually in recent years. If the reform starts with the commercial loan rate, the risk is significant because 80 per cent of all loans will be involved. If the reform fails, the cost will be significant for the same reason. Table 5.3 is a sum balance sheet of all commercial banks in the PRC from 1993 to 1997. Commercial bank loans to enterprises totalled 7069.1 billion Yuan RMB and loans to government were 149.6 billion

Table 5.3   Balance sheet of all banks except People's Bank of China (billion Yuan RMB)

	1993	1994	1995	1996	1997
Asset in foreign countries	67.37	61.27	−29.97	−3.98	99.10
Reserve	583.21	760.11	1009.56	1369.49	1627.48
Reserve	288.77	394.10	524.98	654.56	914.33
Saving at the central bank	240.67	298.18	395.95	651.65	632.80
Cash	53.77	59.56	68.92	63.28	80.35
T-bond	0.00	8.27	19.71	0.00	9.77
Loan for the government	7.45	46.01	104.14	180.43	149.57
Loan for enterprise & other corp.	3089.28	3864.0	4808.6	5823.16	7069.1
Loan for non-financial corp.	0.00	64.50	77.61	77.57	222.40
Liability	2608.77	3567.40	4784.98	6171.57	7530.99
Saving	969.29	1238.99	1520.16	1876.49	2381.03
Time deposit	124.79	194.31	332.42	504.19	673.85
Demand deposit	1458.29	2051.60	2804.55	3637.34	4363.52
Other deposit	56.40	82.50	127.85	153.55	112.59
Liability to government	968.03	1031.65	1117.39	1421.01	1400.29
Liability to non-financial corp.	0.00	35.39	43.70	57.94	150.10
Bonds	22.86	19.57	17.01	28.81	28.65
Owner's right	237.73	291.9	297.04	329.78	331.14
Realized capital	237.73	283.54	261.12	285.60	340.61
Other	−90.08	−150.02	−290.18	−562.44	−263.77

Source: The People's Bank of China, *ACFB* (1998)

Yuan RMB in 1997. The total GDP for the year 1997 was 7314 billion Yuan RMB (Table 3.11 in Chapter 3, p. 83). The commercial banks' loans to enterprises and other corporations were almost equal to GDP in 1997. If reform of interest rates starts with commercial bank loan rates, the impact on the economy will be significant. Commercial bank loan rates ought not to be totally decided by the market in the initial stages of reform.

The risk will be much smaller if the reform of interest rates starts with loans involving foreign currency. This is because foreign currency deposits are only 7 per cent of total deposits, and loans are 6 per cent of total loans. The reform will not have a significant impact on the market. The sequence for interest rates reform is to float the interest rates of foreign currency loans first, and then float the interest rates of foreign currency deposits. Then interest rates of domestic currency loans can be floated and following those, the rates for deposits will be floated. The reforms will be implemented in rural areas first, and then they will be implemented in urban areas.

In China, in 2001, deposits of foreign currency totalled US$117 billion and foreign currency loans granted by commercial banks totalled US$67.5 billion. The sum of the loans was much smaller than the sum of the deposits. Because of this difference, it is reasonable to float the interest rates of foreign currency loans. The significant deposits can be used for future demand for loans if the loan rates are floated.

The PBC gained experience in interest rate control in 1993 when the 'Administration Rules for Interest Rates' was published. All the effective policies that the PBC implemented in 1993 were included. In this document, the PBC clearly indicates that it uses 'interest rates to regulate economic growth'. Interest rates are used as monetary policy tools to reach a long-term target – GDP growth. The PBC is 'the administrator of the interest rate authorized by the State Council' and any group or individual cannot interfere. In the inter-bank lending market, discount market, treasury bill market, bond market and commercial paper market, interest rates are controlled by the PBC and are clearly defined in Chapter 2, Article 5 in 'Administration Rules for Interest Rates'. Chapter 2 Article 6 gives the commercial banks rights to set their own floating rates, intra-bank rates, and inter-bank lending rate. Chapter 2 Articles 7, 8 and 9 define the responsibilities of the PBC, PBC branches, and commercial banks in interest rate regulation. Chapters 3 and 4 state methods by which deposit and loan rates may be calculated. The rules are enforced by the PBC. Any violators will have to pay fines stipulated in Chapter 5 (People's Bank of China, *ACFB*, 1994).

On 21 September 2000, the PRC began to reform the interest rate. The interest rates of foreign currency loans were floated. They will be decided by demand and supply in the markets. The reform will provide good guidance for future interest rate reform of the domestic currency RMB.

The gradual reform of interest rates largely depends on the interest rate feedback signals from the markets. The feedback reflects the market demand. But only when the signals are of high quality, not distorted, can the monetary authority command proper benchmark rates for the markets.

The Chinese money market has not been fully developed yet. The credit concept has not been widely accepted by the public and rejection of financial notes is usual when circulated in the markets. It reflects insufficient public confidence in financial markets, and discounts the quality of the feedback signals of interest rates. The separation of the inter-bank lending market, bond markets, commercial paper markets and the treasury bill markets produces different interest rates for different markets. But the rates have no fixed relationship to each other. China has floated the inter-bank lending rate and treasury bill rate.

According to the current situation, China can test the reforms in the fully developed markets first. For example, the PBC treats the inter-bank lending rates as benchmark rates. This is similar to the Fed fund rate in the United States, treated as one of the benchmark rates largely used by the Federal Reserve Bank as a monetary policy tool.

Then the PRC can gradually reform the discount rate system, using the discount rate as another benchmark rate (Luo, 2001).

The third step might be increasing the range in which the commercial bank loan interest rates can float. This step will allow commercial banks to adjust the commercial loan rates more sensitively in order to maximize profits. Eventually loan rates will reflect the market equilibrium and be more sensitive to the central banks' monetary policy adjustment. The monetary policy will be more effective. The central bank can affect the rates through setting the ceiling of interest rates of commercial loans. The commercial banks can transmit the PBC's message to the market through the commercial loan rates.

6
Empirical Study of Monetary Policy Tools

'Men at some time are masters of their fates.
The fault, dear Brutus, is not in our stars,
But in ourselves, that we are underlings.'

William Shakespeare, *Julius Caesar*, I. ii. 139

6.1 Introduction

This chapter presents an empirical study of effectiveness of the conduct of Chinese monetary policy in the period after the 1993–5 financial system reforms. It was shown in Chapter 4 that the Chinese economy and its currency remained strong throughout the recent Asian Financial Crisis, beginning in July of 1997 and extending through the spring of 1999. It was suggested that the reason for the stability of the Chinese economy during the crisis could be attributed to its soundly re-engineered financial architecture along the lines of the US Glass-Steagall Act of 1933 (now repealed) accomplished during the period of financial reforms in China. It was also suggested that the conduct of sound monetary policy in the post-reform period, particularly during the Asian Financial Crisis, might also have been a contributing factor to the financial stability of the Chinese economy throughout the crisis period. It is the purpose of the empirical study described in this chapter to test this hypothesis.

Chapter 3 pointed out that after 1995 the PBC, having set up a policy channel and associated infrastructure to use open market operations to target monetary aggregates, attempted to use interest rate targets and phase-in monetary targets. But in 1996, the PBC was quickly forced to abandon open market operations, at least temporarily, because of the immaturity of the Chinese treasury market. The treasury market was simply too thin and shallow to be a practical channel for monetary policy at that time. It was re-established in 1998. The PBC had to maintain its focus on interest-rate targets and reserve ratio requirements, but this may have been a good thing, in retrospect, because the interest-rate target regime seemed to work well for China during 1993–7. The appropriateness of an interest rate target versus a money supply target can be tested empirically in the context of a statistical model originally developed by William Poole (1970).

6.2   Theory

In this chapter, a regression model based on the Poole (1970) regressions is used to test the appropriateness of the conduct of monetary policy by the PBC in the post-reform era. The Poole regression model tests for the proper choice of policy instruments in the context of a regression model in the form of the *IS-LM* framework developed by Hicks (1937). In theory and practice, a monetary authority must choose operation through an interest rate target or a money supply target, but not both. This is primarily due to the fact that money demand shifts cause a divergence of interest rates consistent with an interest-rate or money-supply target independently.

The Hicksian *IS-LM* model is graphically represented by the diagram in Figure 6.1. The *IS* curve represents the various combinations of interest rates (r) and full employment income (Y) for which the goods market clears, and *LM* the various combinations of interest rates (r) and full employment income (Y) for which the money market clears.

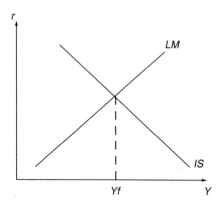

Figure 6.1   IS-LM model

An interest-rate target (r^*) would be depicted as a horizontal *LM* curve, as depicted in Figure 6.2.

The issue of whether an interest rate target or a monetary target would be more appropriate depends upon which market is more unstable, the goods market or the money market. An unstable goods market is represented by shifts in the *IS* curve as it is randomly shocked, as shown in Figure 6.3.

In Figure 6.3 a money supply target (M^*) is depicted as a stable LM_1. If the goods market is relatively unstable compared with the money market, the *IS* curve shifts between IS_1 and IS_2 and a stable LM_1 applies (there is no interest-rate target). So if the *IS* curve is randomly shocked, and there is no interest rate target, then income ranges between Y_1 and Y_2. But with an interest rate target (r^*), LM_2 would then apply, and income would range between Y_0 and Y_3, which is a wider range of income than between Y_1 and Y_2. So a money supply target (M^*) would be superior to an interest rate target (r^*) when the goods market is relatively unstable compared to the money market, because income ranges less with a money supply target.

In the situation in which the money market is relatively unstable compared to the goods market, the reverse would be true. A relatively unstable money market would be depicted as shifts in the *LM* curve as it is randomly shocked as shown in Figure 6.4.

If the central bank sets a money supply target (M^*), and the money market is relatively unstable compared with the goods market, the *LM*

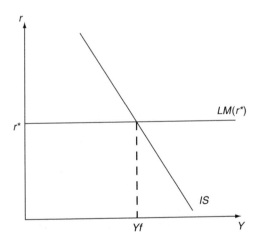

Figure 6.2 IS-LM model with an interest-rate target (r^*)

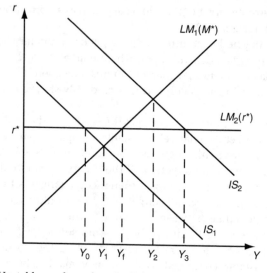

Figure 6.3 Unstable goods market: the *IS* function is randomly shocked and may lie anywhere between IS_1 and IS_2

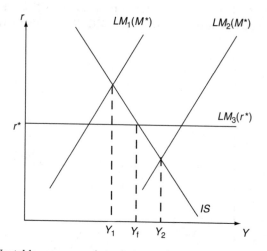

Figure 6.4 Unstable money market relative to the goods market: the *IS* function is stable but the money demand function is randomly shocked between LM_1 and LM_2

curve shifts between LM_1 and LM_2 and a stable *IS* curve applies (there is no interest rate target). So if the *LM* curve is randomly shocked, and there is no interest rate target, then income ranges between Y_1 and Y_2. But had we set an interest rate target (r^*), instead of a money supply target (M^*), LM_3 would apply consistent with interest rate target (r^*), just as in the case of Figure 6.2. In this case, income would be stable at Y_f. So in the case in which the money market is more unstable than the goods market, an interest rate target would be superior for the central bank to choose in making decisions.

6.3 The model

It would appear from the *IS-LM* analysis, as depicted in Figures 6.2 and 6.3, that the answer to the question of which policy tool to use, an interest rate target or a monetary target, would depend on the relative stability of the goods market compared with the money market. This, in turn, would depend on the relative importance of the random disturbances, and on the slopes of the *IS* and *LM* curves. Poole (1970) developed a model to test for the choice of monetary policy tool by estimating a stochastic *IS* and *LM* curve, and analysing the structural parameters of the system.

Poole's model is composed of two equations, for an *IS* and *LM* curve, respectively. The two-equation model is given by equations 6.1 and 6.2, where Y is real GDP, r is the operational interest rate target, and M is a monetary aggregate. Equation 6.1 represents the *IS* curve, and equation 6.2 represents the *LM* curve. In equation 6.1, coefficient a_1 must be negative because the *IS* curve always downward-sloping and investment demand is inversely related to interest rates. In equation 6.2, coefficient b_1 represents the income elasticity of money demand, which should be positive because transactions demand is positive. Coefficient b_2 represents the interest elasticity of money demand, and is therefore negative because of the opportunity cost of holding money when interest rates are high:

$$\ln Y = a_0 + a_1 \ln r + e_1 \qquad\qquad a_1 < 0 \quad \text{IS curve} \qquad (6.1)$$

$$\ln M = b_0 + b_1 \ln Y + b_2 \ln r + e_2 \quad b_1 > 0, \quad b_2 < 0 \quad \text{LM curve} \qquad (6.2)$$

The implication of the Poole model, as described by equations 6.1 and 6.2, is that the success of a monetary policy initiative is related to the benefit to the economy that results from the implementation of the policy, which can be measured relative to the particular level of desired national income. So the selection of an appropriate policy instrument depends on which instrument minimizes the loss from failing to reach that desired level of national income. Poole thus analyses the choice of policy instrument by determining the minimum expected loss using a quadratic loss function along the lines of Theil (1964), and shows that the higher the interest sensitivity of the demand for money (the lower b_2 is algebraically, or the more negative b_2 is), the lower the expected loss from a monetary-target policy. So, practically speaking, a relatively low value for b_2 (the more negative) means the monetary authority should use a money supply target, and a relatively high value for b_2 (the less negative compared with -1) means that the monetary authority should go with an interest rate target. This will be the operational criterion, hereafter referred to as the Poole criterion, for the analysis of the appropriate policy regime.

In this chapter the Poole model is implemented in the following way. The regression model described by the Poole equations 6.1 and 6.2 are estimated by ordinary least squares (OLS) regression techniques, using macroeconomic data obtained from the PBC for the relevant variables as described below. In this chapter the focus is on the second equation of the Poole model, equation 6.2, which represents the *LM* curve. We are not interested in the first equation, equation 6.1, because it represents the *IS* curve. The *IS* curve embodies fiscal policy, which was stable throughout the period of the study, and is, in any case, not the focus of this study. The analysis of the appropriate monetary policy instrument is therefore based on the estimate of the regression coefficients of the second equation of the Poole model, equation 6.2, using the Poole criterion as described above.

6.4   Data: sources and methods

A database was assembled consisting of quarterly real GDP, the 20–day Chinese discount rate, M0 (currency outstanding), M1, and M2 for the period 1986 to 1999. GDP and money supply (M0, M1, and M2) are reported in billions of Yuan, and obtained from the *Almanac of China's Finance and Banking*, published by the PBC (People's Bank of China, *ACFB*, 1994–9, 2000). Real GDP data are calculated from nominal GDP and the GDP deflator, contained in the *China Statistics Yearbook*. Data for the 20-day Chinese discount rates are also obtained from the *Almanac of China's Finance and Banking*. Data for monetary aggregates, such as M0 (currency outstanding), M1, and M2 are obtained from the PBC's *China Monthly Statistics Summary*, and reported in billions of Yuan RMB.

6.5 Estimation

The regression model given by equation 6.2 was estimated by the ordinary least squares (OLS) method in two separate regressions for a split data sample for the period prior to and the period subsequent to the 1993–5 reforms: 1986 through 1994, and 1995 through the second quarter of 1999. The results of these regressions are reported below, in equations 6.3 and 6.4 respectively.

In the first regression model, equation 6.2 was first estimated by OLS for the period 1986 through 1994. In order to correct for serial correlation in these data, it was necessary to estimate the first period regression using the generalized least squares (GLS) method, to correct for autocorrelation using an AR-1 process. The model was estimated separately using three monetary aggregates M0, M1 and M2. The best results are obtained for M0, followed by M1 and M2. Apparently, for the Chinese economy, the most relevant measure of the money supply is outstanding currency (M0). It would seem that because the Chinese financial system is still developing, but as yet immature, most Chinese citizens still conduct most of their financial transactions in cash, not holding much wealth in the form of chequing accounts or time deposits. The results of the first period regression are reported below in equation 6.3:

$$\ln M_0 = 6.415361 - 0.09272 \ln Y + 0.00509 \ln r \qquad (6.3)$$

$$t \qquad (7.840) \qquad (-1.537) \qquad (0.026)$$

$$P \qquad [0.000] \qquad [0.124] \qquad [0.979]$$

$$F[2, 33] = 36.65 \quad \text{Adjusted } R^2 = 0.6707 \quad DW = 1.4119$$

The results for the first period regression (6.3) are not good. Although the overall model is significant to the zero probability level, based on the F-statistic, adjusted R^2 is not high, only 67 per cent, and the t-statistics are not particularly good on the slope coefficients. The numbers in parentheses are the t-statistics and the numbers in brackets are the probability levels for the significance of the coefficients. Moreover, we get the wrong signs for the coefficients on the log of income and the log of the interest rate. The signs should be reversed, positive on the income elasticity and negative on the interest rate elasticity.

These 'bad' results are attributed to 'bad' monetary policy in the pre-reform era. Neither interest rate targeting nor monetary targeting was implemented until after the reforms, starting in 1993. The Chinese were still using the old credit plan, which amounted to state-directed credit, which did not have a monetary policy component. So these results are not entirely unexpected for the first period.

The real issue is what happened after the reforms and the conduct of monetary policy. Was the post-reform monetary policy regime successful? To answer this question equation 6.2 was estimated a second time by OLS for the period 1995 through the second quarter of 1999. The results for the second period regression are reported below in equation 6.4:

$$ln\, M0 = 6.198004 + 0.168432\, ln\, Y - 0.405296\, ln\, r \qquad (6.4)$$

$$t \qquad (7.788) \qquad (1.960) \qquad (-6.288)$$

$$P \qquad [0.0000] \qquad [0.06882] \qquad [0.00001]$$

$$F[2,15] = 30.63 \quad \text{Adjusted } R^2 = 0.777 \quad DW = 1.19759$$

The results for the second period regression 6.4 are very good. The overall model is significant to the zero probability level, based on the F-statistic, and adjusted R^2 is a much higher value of 78 per cent. The t-statistics for the estimated coefficients are all highly significant, and the coefficients on the log of income and on the log of interest rate are both of the correct sign. Also, the coefficient on the log of the interest rate is relatively high (less negative compared with -1), indicating that the interest-rate target policy instrument would have been most appropriate for China during this period, based on the Poole model criterion.

The negative correlation between the interest rate and the money supply indicates that the money supply will be tight when the discount rate is high. This indicates that the monetary authorities can refer to the discount rate to get an idea of the current situation of the money supply and demand, and then decide to increase or decrease the money supply.

A relatively high (significantly less than -1) coefficient on the log of the interest-rate variable indicates that the interest-rate sensitivity of money demand in China during this period was relatively low. This minimizes the loss associated with the choice of an interest-rate target policy instrument. So an interest-rate target policy would have been most appropriate for China during this period, which was the case during the post-reform period. And this is borne out by the good statistical results obtained for the second period regression.

Hence, the statistical results obtained from the split sample regression study indicate that the PBC's monetary policy committee should have chosen an interest-rate target rather than a monetary target, as it did. A money supply target would have been inappropriate for China during this period. This is because the Chinese money market was relatively unstable compared to the goods market. Under these circumstances the *IS-LM* analytical framework, as depicted in Figure 6.4, indicates that an interest rate target is superior to a money supply target.

In the post-reform period, the Chinese economy grew at a steady pace of 7–10 per cent, with low inflation. The inflation rate dropped to only 3 per cent per annum by 1996. These conditions contributed to an environment of relative stability in Chinese goods markets. On the other hand, conditions in Chinese money markets were unstable. Before the reforms, only the large financial institutions in China, which included the four big commercial banks and the provincial investment and trust companies, could invest in stocks and bonds. But after the reforms ordinary citizens had access to these investments. Moreover, the Chinese people conduct most of their daily transactions in cash. This is because their financial services sector is still immature, and ordinary citizens do not hold chequing accounts or hold credit cards. So Chinese citizens either hold cash or invest in stocks and bonds. And because Chinese bond and equity markets are still thin and shallow, the interest rate sensitivity of the demand for money is low. So an interest rate target is more appropriate for China under these economic and financial conditions.

Thus, as a result of the serious study and practice of monetary policy, the Chinese central bank chose the right policy instrument. In the post-reform era, the central bank had attempted to phase-in monetary targets through open market operations along with interest rate targets. But because of the immaturity of the Chinese government securities market, they were forced to abandon open market operation until very recently. So the central bank, much by accident, was forced to use interest rate targeting only, which turned out to be the right prescription. Poole (1970) and others have shown that simultaneous interest-rate and monetary targets do not work in any case.

It is worth pointing out that the Chinese monetary authority depended almost exclusively on a money supply channel for the conduct of its monetary policy before 1993, but had already abandoned monetary targeting in favour of interest rate targeting in the second half of 1993. Monetary targeting had been accomplished by issuing credit to local banks and by extending the administration of loan quotas to specific industries. Monetary policy was implemented through a credit channel. Part of the 1992 economic reforms initiated by Deng Xiaoping's trip to several cities in the South China emphasized the extension of state-directed credit towards both public and private sector investment to stimulate development. This resulted in a real estate bubble which led to severe inflation by 1993 (the monthly inflation rate in China ran between 13 and 50 per cent throughout 1993), and so the effort needed to be abandoned. The Chinese central bank needed to raise interest rates to curb inflation, attract savings, and reduce disintermediation by depositors who had been receiving low rates on savings deposits. So the central bank began to focus on an interest rate policy. Thereafter, the interest rate became the primary monetary policy tool of the central bank. This policy worked quite well for China before the 1995 reforms had been completely implemented. Hence, the failed attempt to embark on a dual policy regime, with simultaneous interest-rate and monetary targeting, in favour of interest rate targeting only after the reforms, may have been fortuitous for China.

6.6   Further research

In order to discuss further the data collected in the regression model above, Figure 6.5 shows the relationship of GDP, interest and money supply (M2).

The positive correlation between the money supply and the real GDP (Figure 6.5) fits the economic theory that the increase of the money supply has a stimulating effect on economic growth. It is worth pointing out that money supply (M2) growth was bigger than GDP growth after 1995 (see Figure 6.5). The 'gap' between M2 and GDP becomes significant in recent years, and it is becoming greater. This phenomenon suggests that the PBC's use of money supply as one of the monetary policy tools might have had less impact on GDP growth in recent years than before 1995. The reason might be that PBC has to allocate extra funds to pay for the increased overdue loans and default loans. The achievements of the four asset management corporations have not been included as this is too recent. They may help to reduce the gap between M2 and GDP in the future.

Another reason for the increase in the gap between M2 and GDP might be the 'idle cash' problem discussed in Chapter 5 (p. 117). Commercial banks are reluctant to grant new loans because of fear of default. Individuals and households are hesitant to invest in the stock market because Chinese stock markets are not completely mature. Thus, large amounts of funds are held by commercial banks as 'idle cash' and largely discount the effects of the PBC's money supply increase. The 'idle cash' problem in China will decrease the effect of open market operations if not properly solved.

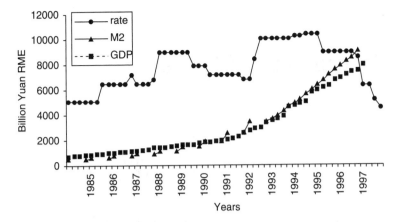

Figure 6.5 GDP, interest rate and money supply (M2)
Sources: China Statistics Yearbook, various issues; People's Bank of China (1993–9), *Almanac of China's Finance and Banking*, various issues.

Figure 6.5 also shows that between 1992 and 1995 the gap between M2 and GDP is not significant. During this period, interest rate adjustment was implemented by the PBC to control inflation in 1992–3. The PBC did not conduct open market operations. The government's stimulation between 1992 and the first half of 1993 caused the increase of investments. The 'idle cash' problem was not significant. All the above might contribute to the explanation of the disappeared gap between M2 and GDP. The disappeared gap suggests GDP growth may be more sensitive to the money supply change. The smaller the gap between M2 and GDP, the more sensitive the economy is in response to monetary policy. If this is true, the PBC's monetary policy between 1992 and 1995 should have more significant impact on the Chinese economy during this period than in other periods. In fact, the interest rate cut in the second half of 1993 did increase savings deposits dramatically and decrease the inflation rate significantly. For future study, data in other countries might be needed to illustrate the relationship between M2 and GDP and its policy implication for the conduct of monetary policy.

7
Conclusions and Suggestions

'Too swift arrives as tardy as too slow.'

William Shakespeare, *Romeo and Juliet*, II. vi. 15

7.1 Introduction

This study is an analysis of banking reforms in China between 1978 and 2000 and the Chinese central bank's conduct of monetary policy by control of interest rates, reserve ratio requirements and open market operations. China experienced four periods of sequential monetary policy reforms. It has been shown in this book that, following the 1978–2000 reforms, the Chinese banking system was put on a sound financial footing. Challenges that the Chinese banking system will face after China's joining of the World Trade Organization include supervision of foreign banks, financial risks, the default loan issue and the bankruptcy issue.

7.2 Analysis of Chinese banking reform

Before 1978 China had the monopoly bank that had sole responsibility for accepting savings deposits and disseminating industrial and commercial credit in the form of government-directed loans. The bank also served as the sole network for the distribution of currency, and the formulation and conduct of monetary policy.

After spinning off commercial banking and policy banking businesses, the PBC became an independent central bank. Conducting monetary policy is one of its major responsibilities and the PBC was given a clear monetary policy role. The tools to implement this role include exclusive control over the setting of interest rates, reserve ratio requirements, the creation of an inter-bank money market, and the implementation of open market operations. In the period from 1978 to 1994, free movement of foreign currency was forbidden and exchange rates were set by the central bank, maintenance of exchange stability was not the monetary policy target. Instead, the monetary policy target was control of inflation and the growth of the economy.

In January 1995 exchange rate restrictions were removed. The maintenance of a stable exchange rate became one of the PBC's monetary policy targets. In 1995 the PBC tested open market operations, but because of the immaturity of the Chinese government securities market they were forced to abandon open market operations until very recently. So the central bank, much by accident, was forced to use interest-rate targeting only, which turned out to be the right prescription for China in 1993–7. The PBC also used reserve ratio requirements as another monetary policy tool.

Before 1 January 1998 China still used loan ceilings to control domestic demand. The credit plan and cash plan were used by the PBC to control credit. The initial design of control of credit was based on allocation of difference between deposits and loans granted. The branches which have surplus deposits have to submit the surplus deposits to PBC. The central bank (PBC) controls the money supply by control of loans granted by the commercial banks.

In 1998 loan ceilings were removed. Open market operations were re-established at the end of 1998 because the Chinese treasury market became more liquid. The PBC depends on open market operations to reach monetary policy targets indirectly and to control commercial loans indirectly. The removal of the loan ceilings was based on the confidence in the PBC's experience in the conduct of monetary policy. The experience came from the central banking reforms of the previous two decades. The money supply has been used as one of the major tools to conduct monetary policy since then.

The result of the reforms has been the stable growth of economy. GDP growth rate was 6–12 per cent in the last two decades. Moreover, China was insulated from most parts of the Asian Financial Crisis in 1997. The Chinese were able to maintain a stable exchange rate of 8.29 Yuan RMB per US dollar throughout the crisis. The GDP grew 7.8 per cent in 1998. It appears that a collapse of the Chinese currency was not possible during the crisis. China's foreign exchange reserve remained strong throughout the period. It grew consistently from the second quarter of 1997 through to the second quarter of 1998.

7.3 The findings

The Poole model

To verify whether those achievements were due to the conduct of sound monetary policy in China, the Chinese central bank's choice of policy instruments being used to stabilize the economy throughout the crisis period were examined empirically in the context of a statistical model developed by William Poole (1970). The empirical study shows that F-statistics and t-statistics are all highly significant, and the coefficients on the log of income and on the log of interest rate are both of the correct sign. The coefficient on the log of the interest rate is relatively high, indicating that the interest-rate target policy instrument would have been most appropriate for China during 1993–7, based on the Poole model criterion.

This lends credence to the hypothesis that the conduct of sound monetary policy, in addition to the structural banking reforms, indeed contributed to the stable Chinese economy during this period.

Development of Chinese monetary policy in five periods in 1949–2002

According to the International Conference on the Monetary Policy in May 2001, the PBC is preparing to use the modern theory of the monetary policy transit mechanism to set up a sensitive and effective mechanism for monetary policy. The ideal monetary policy will be changing the intermediate target from controlling money supply to the long-term interest rate. Money supply as the monetary policy tool will eventually be replaced by the short-term interest rate. In the transition time during the reform, the monetary policy transit mechanism will depend on the quantity parameter – the money supply. The interest rate – the price parameter – will be a supplementary factor. As the money market matures, the mechanism will change from the quantity parameter to the price parameter. China has already built the monetary policy transit channel of 'the PBC → Money Market → Financial Institution → Enterprise'. And China has also built the indirect transit channel of 'Policy Tool → Operating Target → Intermediate Target → Target (International Conference on Monetary Policy, 2001).

To summarize the overall development of the PBC monetary policy described in this book, a five-period model can be introduced as shown in Table 7.1. In this model, the monetary policy in Chinese history was divided into five periods according to the differences in the monetary policy transit mechanism.

Table 7.1 Five-period model of Chinese monetary policy and its transition mechanism

	Before reform (1949–78)	After reform but under the foreign exchange restriction period (1978–94)	Floating exchange rate & direct monetary policy (1995–8)	Indirect monetary policy (1998–2002)	After joining WTO (some proposals) (2002–)
Monetary policy tools	Credit plan Cash plan Administration	Interest rate Discount rate Special deposit (H. Wang, 2001) Loan ceiling	Reserve requirement Discount rate Open market operation (OMO)[1]	Reserve requirement Discount rate Open market operation	From open market operation to interest rate (Discount rate, inter-bank lending rate); Reserve requirement
Intermediate target	Four balances (H. Wang, 2001)	Loan ceiling	Money supply[2] Loan ceiling[3]	Money supply	Money supply Other
Target	GDP growth Inflation	From GDP growth and inflation to money supply	Money supply Exchange rate GDP growth	Money supply Exchange rate GDP growth	Money supply Exchange rate GDP growth

[1]OMO was tested for a short period of time in 1995 then stopped. It was re-established in 1998.
[2]Money supply was in place from 1995 till now.
[3]In this period, loan ceiling was in place from 1995 to 1997 and ceased on 1 Jan. 1998.

Before the economic reform (1949–78), China adopted the banking system of the former Soviet Union, that is, a centrally planned economy. The PBC acted as a government agency regulated by the Ministry of Finance. Monetary policies were conducted through the credit plan and the cash plan by administration orders. From 1978 to 1994 the PBC, as the central bank, began monetary policy implementation. Researchers have questioned the use of the interest rate policy in 1993 as a monetary policy tool by the PBC. Some authors think that the Chinese SOEs are largely inelastic to the interest rate because of the government subsidy and PBC's lack of knowledge of the interest rate operation in monetary policy decision-making. Those authors think China did not have any experience in the use of the discount rate as a monetary policy tool before 2001. Whether it can be tested in the short term still remains questionable (H. Wang, 2001). We argue that the PBC used the interest rates (discount rate, savings deposit rate and loan rate) as microeconomic tools to control inflation in 1993. The outcome was very good. The use of the interest rate tool and other practices successfully allowed a 'soft landing'. These practices prevented the 1997 Asian Financial Crisis from affecting the Chinese economy. In 1993, as discussed in earlier chapters, the PBC adjusted the interest rates (including the discount rate) three times (in April, May and July of 1993). This was a total increase of 342 basis points within four months. Alan Greenspan of the US Federal Reserve increased the interest rates in 2000 and then slashed the rates in 2001. The sizes and frequency of the 1993 interest rate changes in China are comparable to those of the United States.

During this period of 1978–94, the PBC inherited some aspects of the central planned economy that included loan ceilings limiting the ability of commercial banks to grant loans. In addition, the special deposit by the PBC in the commercial banks also acted as one of the monetary policy tools, according to H. Wang (2001).

In the period between 1978 and 1994 the open market operation was not treated as a monetary policy tool because China had strict foreign currency control. During this period free foreign exchange was forbidden. The PBC's creation of monetary policy was influenced neither by the trade balance nor by exchange rate stability. The monetary policy tools used were interest rates. The money supply tool was not useful because of the immature inter-bank lending market and government bond market. The monetary policy target was GDP growth and inflation without considering the exchange rate.

After 1994 China reformed the foreign exchange management to allow the exchange rate to float within a certain range. There are no more restrictions on the free exchange of foreign currencies. Starting from 1995, monetary policy began to consider the international trade balance, foreign currency assets, and liabilities in the banks. The exchange rate became the target (H. Wang, 2001). The open market operation became one of the major tools for the PBC.

In 1998, loan ceiling ceased. Banks have more flexibility in granting loans. The reserve requirements were reduced from 13 per cent to 8 per cent in 1998 and from 8 per cent to 6 per cent in 1999. Open market operations played an active role in the controlling of deflation from the late 1990s to the present time. The discount rate was continually utilized as a monetary policy tool. The monetary policy target was stability of the exchange rate, and GDP growth.

To prevent conflict of interest, commercial banking operations and investment banking operations are separated in China. This separation prevents commercial banks from speculating in the stock market and depositors' savings are protected. It creates a division between the two kinds of banks which is similar to that instituted by the Glass-Steagall Act of 1933 of the United States.

McKinnon and Shaw (McKinnon, 1973; Shaw, 1973) proposed an endogenous growth theory, which we found fits the Chinese case very well. Even though financial liberalization affects savings, investment and income, it indirectly affects steady-state rate of growth, which is largely determined by exogenous technical progress. In China, financial developments seem to have a big and immediate impact on GDP growth. The technical progress in the period between 1978 and 1992 (before banking system reform) was the same as that of the period between 1993 and 2002. There was a big difference in economic development. The above seems to support the theory proposed by Arestis *et al.* (Arestis and Demetriades, 1999):

> There can be self-sustaining growth without exogenous technical progress. While individual firms may be faced with declining returns-to-scale, their efficiency may depend on the aggregate capital stock. Capital accumulation may trigger a learning process and could, therefore, be considered as a public good that raises overall efficiency in the economy.

Since China joined the WTO at the end of 2001, there came the fifth period of the Chinese monetary policy development. Regarding the new challenges that Chinese banks face after China's entry of WTO, some proposals are raised as follows.

7.4 The proposals for permitting stock-backed collateral loans

It is proposed that the investment banks may be granted stock-backed collateral loans by the commercial banks. Free movement of funds between the commercial bank and the investment bank will be permitted.

Money enters the stock markets in several ways. Commercial bank loans are granted to stockbrokers using stocks or bonds as collateral. On 13 February 2000, the PBC published the 'Regulation of Loans by Securities Firms with Stock as Collateral'. It provides a guideline for legal fund-raising for the securities firms. Another source of money for investment banks is inter-bank borrowing directly from the commercial banks. By mid-2001, 12 stockbrokers and 10 fund management companies were allowed to participate in the inter-bank lending market. Inter-bank borrowing is convenient and quick. It is an ideal way for the securities firms to get short-term funds. The third source of funds is the state-owned, state-controlled or public companies which invest in the stock markets.

There are also some indirect ways for commercial banking funds to enter the stock market. Some loans are transferred from a company to its parent holding company, then it is invested into the stock market. Or some enterprises put the loans into trust accounts or fund management accounts in securities firms. The securities firms then purchase stock with the fund. Another indirect way is called the 'crossing bridge loan' meaning that enterprises put some cash in the stockbroker's account as collateral, the stockbroker provide guarantees for the enterprises to get loans from the commercial banks. Then the loan enters into the stock brokerage firms to purchase stocks. Other indirect ways include private consumption loan entering into the stock markets, enterprises transferring funds into private accounts to invest in the stock markets. Enterprises purchase bonds or become board members of a securities firm.

There is a positive side to the use of commercial loans to buy stocks. When the central bank increases the money supply, more loans can be granted. When the loans are invested in the stock market, they will stimulate growth of the economy. This is one way the central bank can control the growth of the economy through the use of the money supply. The stock market is sensitive to the money supply when loans can be used to buy stocks. In the United States, the stock markets are also sensitive to monetary policy changes. For example, each time Alan Greenspan announced the Federal Reserve monetary policy in 2000, the New York Stock Exchange and the NASDAQ market reacted immediately.

Since the security firms can get loans from the commercial banks by using the stock shares as collateral in China, the newly acquired loans will probably be utilized to purchase more stocks. The new stocks can be used as new collateral in order to get more loans from the commercial banks. This cycle will amplify the effect of loans, and eventually amplify the effect of the central bank's monetary policy. Moreover, the stock-backed collateral loans will cause the capital market and the money market be more closely linked. The stock-backed collateral loans flow into the capital market, in other words more and more money will flow into the stock market. The stock prices will rise. The enterprises can raise more funds through the securities markets. The commercial banks have more enthusiasm to make new loans, thus increasing the interest income. By the end of 2000, the total market capitalization of both Shanghai and Shenzhen stock exchange markets was about US$193 billion. If 15 per cent of stock values are used for collateral, more than $28 billion may be borrowed and invested in the stock markets. This will dramatically improve both the commercial banks' interest income and the enterprises' fund raising in the stock markets.

Theoretically, when the stock-backed collateral loans from a commercial bank are invested in the stock market, the commercial bank can get interest income from granting loans. The stock price will rise. The commercial banks will grant more loans to enterprises and securities firms. Enterprises will invest more in production, research and development, and as a result will become more profitable. The increased profitability of enterprises will attract more investors. The securities firms also invest loans in the enterprise stocks. The small and middle-sized companies can easily raise funds in the stock market and can use the raised funds to improve their management. Unfortunately, it is possible that some badly managed companies will misuse the funds raised from the stock market. Some companies may be encouraged to manipulate their accounts in order to push their stock price high. This is the theory of adverse selection. However, this defect is not created by the stock-backed collateral loans. It will still exist even though there are no such loans. This is the issue which should be considered in the financial supervision arena by the monetary policy authority.

The increased funds in the stock market generated by the stock-backed collateral loans affect the consumer's asset holding structure. People not only have interest income from savings, but also hold stocks, the values of which could increase more quickly than savings. This positive prospect for future wealth will stimulate consumption. The consumer product industry will grow more quickly.

From the financial intermediary's point of view, more funds are channelled into the stock market. Enterprises can raise funds directly from the stock market. It will make the commercial banks' role decline in enterprise fund-raising. The other kinds of financial intermediary such as investment banks and brokerage firms will play more active roles in the economy. The experience of the developed countries showed that increased competition among financial intermediaries and diversification of the enterprise fund-raising increased the efficiency of the economy. In addition, the financial policy innovations such as allowing private consumption loans, stock-backed collateral loans and the security firms entering the money market will promote active interaction between the monetary authority and the markets. It will make the monetary policy change more sensitive to markets. Eventually it will help the Chinese central bank to change its monetary policy tools from the money supply to interest rates.

The cooperation between commercial banking and investment banking in China will be established because they both need each other. Commercial banks need the services provided by investment banks such as client reserve cash and operating funds. They also need the investment banks' analysts to investigate company management and operation and fund-operating information. Investment banks need the resources of commercial banks such as the clearing system, fund-raising channels, the retail banking network and client information.

Facing such a challenge, the Chinese commercial banks can act by expanding their traditional business into new and riskier areas of lending in order to get higher returns. In the United States banks have put some funds into commercial real estate loans. In addition, they have increased lending for corporate takeovers and leveraged buyouts, which are highly leveraged transaction loans (Mishkin, 1998). In China, this happened in 1992–3 when the branches of the four commercial banks in the south and south-east coastal areas invested heavily in real estate projects. When later in mid-1993 it contributed to inflation, the PBC started to cool the economy and raised another wave of central banking reform, as stated earlier.

7.5 Proposal for prevention of financial risks

After studying several documents, a number of proposals are made on prevention of financial risks, including the establishment of strict standards for the granting of new loans, the increased flow of money in and out of the banks, the maintainance of a good credit rating by the bank, and building a market-oriented financial intermediary.

China will introduce more rigid standards for the granting of new loans. This change in standards will result in loans of better quality, and decrease the default risks. If there are too many default loans, there will be significant losses to the banks. They will be reluctant to grant new loans. Even companies with good credit will not be able to obtain loans. When companies cannot get funds for production, there is limited production, and finally GDP growth will suffer.

Increase of money flow in and out of the banks will increase the cash circulation ability of banks and will stimulate economic growth. Depositors must be guaranteed funds if they need them. If commercial banks cannot invest in the stock markets, there is less risk for the depositors. No matter what reform is done to the financial system, banks must maintain good credit for the customers. This is a psychological issue for the public. Savings deposits must be able to be repaid. Even a single 'bad' case could harm the bank's trustworthiness, which has been built up over past decades.

Creating a market-oriented financial intermediary will place China in a good financial position. The central bank will supervise the system effectively. State-owned and non-state-owned banks will be supervised by the PBC. Technical operations, micro-regulations and any other monetary policies cannot replace the importance of building a market-oriented system.

7.6 Proposal for the supervision of the illegal money flow into the stock markets from the commercial banks

The PBC has already published the 'Prevention of Commercial Bank Funds Illegally Flowing into the Stock Market' regulation. The 'Securities Market Act' Article 133 and the 'Commercial Bank's Act' (Appendix) Article 40 and Article 46 had already given a conceptual outline of this subject. However, it is not sufficiently detailed to be applied to a specific case. Here are some new proposals.

The PBC and the SEC in China shall set up an electronic information management system to dynamically supervise the money flow from the commercial banks to the stock markets. The commercial banks' balance sheets shall be reviewed more frequently and dynamically. The risk management of both commercial banks and security firms shall be reinforced. The financial-risk alert system shall be responsible for warning of potential bank failure.

The registration regulation in the accounting system shall require the commercial banks and security firms to register every large volume of cash flow into the security market if it is directly or indirectly from the commercial banks.

Nonetheless, all these proposals may contribute to the gradual reform of Chinese financial system, especially of the central banking monetary policy. Optimum order is needed in financial liberalization (McKinnon, 1993) as well as optimum speed, not changing too fast, nor too slowly: 'Too swift arrives as tardy as too slow' (Shakespeare, *Romeo and Juliet*, II. vi. 15). What is the optimum order in the banking reforms? Even McKinnon cannot be sure of the reform sequence as a universal rule for all developing countries. China seems to be on the right track and right pace for reform. Chinese experiences will prove invaluable to other developing countries and can be further examined by economists in order to develop more matured economic theories of financial liberalization.

Appendix 1   The Commercial Banks Act of the People's Republic of China: Legislation Passed by People's Congress, 10 May 1995*

Chapter 1   General

1. The purpose of this Act is to protect the legal rights of: commercial banks, depositors and other customers; to standardize commercial banking operations; to improve loan quality; to reinforce financial supervision; and to discipline financial markets so as to develop a market economy.
2. To define commercial banks as institutions that collect deposits, make loans, and settle payments between industrial enterprises.
3. Responsibilities
    (i) Collect deposits;
    (ii) Issue short-term, medium-term and long-term loans;
    (iii) Settle domestic and international payments;
    (iv) Issue checking accounts;
    (v) Issue bonds;
    (vi) Act as a representative of the Chinese government to cash and issue T-bills, T-notes, and T-bonds to the public;
    (vii) Buy and sell T-bills, T-notes, and T-bonds for their own accounts;
    (viii) Make inter-bank loans;
    (ix) Buy and sell foreign currency;
    (x) Supply credit and collateral for industrial enterprises;
    (xi) Settle payments between industrial enterprises;
    (xii) Provide vault storage space to private individuals and industrial enterprises;
    (xiii) Conduct other business authorized by the People's Bank of China not specified in this act.
4. Commercial banks must assume responsibility for risk of loss, profitability, safety, and liquidity, and manage themselves independently [from The People's Bank of China]. Commercial banks shall do business according to the law without any interference from any person or organization. Commercial banks shall independently take legal responsibility in lawsuits.
5. Business between commercial banks and clients shall be conducted according to equal opportunity, customer willingness, non-discrimination and trust.

---

* Translation from *ACFB* for research purposes only.

Appendix (*continued*)

6. Commercial banks shall guarantee the legal rights of depositors.
7. Commercial bank loans shall made in accordance with the creditworthiness of borrowers and the banks must do their best to make sure that the loans can be repaid. Commercial banks have the right to collect the matured principal plus interest on loans under the protection of law.
8. Commercial banks shall do business according to law and shall not do harm to the national interest and public security.
9. Commercial banks shall compete fairly with each other and shall not engage in unfair competition.
10. Commercial banks shall be supervised by the People's Bank of China.

Chapter 2   Chartering and organizing the commercial banks

11. Commercial banks shall be chartered only by the People's Bank of China. Otherwise, no organization or person shall conduct commercial banking business such as collecting savings deposits. Any other organization must not use the term 'bank' in their names.
12. The chartering of commercial banks shall have the following prerequisites:
    (i) Internal management rules must conform with the 'Act of The People's Bank of China' and 'The Commercial Bank Act of the People's Republic of China'.
    (ii) Capital above the minimum capital requirement defined by this Act.
    (iii) A Chairman, Chief Executive Officer and other officials who have professional knowledge and banking experience.
    (iv) Complete organizational structures and management rules.
    (v) Offices and a safe environment, which meets the required standards. The People's Bank of China shall consider economic development needs and competitive banking conditions when processing applications chartering commercial banks.
13. The minimum bank capital requirement for chartering a new commercial bank is 1 billion RMB.
14. When applying for a commercial bank charter, applicants shall hand in the following documents to the People's Bank of China.
    (i) An application form which includes the name of the commercial bank, its location, capital and business type.
    (ii) Applicable research reports.
    (iii) Other documents as required by the People's Bank of China.
15. After being approved for the first step for chartering in accordance with Article 14, the applicant shall submit a formal application form, which shall include:
    (i) A document explaining internal management rules;
    (ii) Copies of the officers licences for the top management of the bank and other relevant professional certificates.

(iii) Government approved certificate of the proof for the chartered bank's capital.

(iv) A list of major shareholders.

(v) The credit history for the shareholders holding more than 10 per cent of the commercial bank's stock [the major shareholders].

(vi) A statement of the bank's growth targets and plans [for achieving them].

(vii) A description of the office locations and security system.

(viii) Other documents as required by the People's Bank of China.

16. The approved commercial bank will be issued a management permit by the People's Bank of China.

17. The organization of the banks shall be in accordance with the Company Organization Act of the People's Republic of China.

18. State-owned commercial banks shall have an audit committee consisting of representatives from the People's Bank of China, the central government, regulatory organizations and the bank itself. The audit committee shall audit the state-owned commercial banks' loan quality, balance sheet, state assets and management, and prevent the bank from conducting illegal operations.

19. The commercial banks may establish local branches and foreign branches with the permission of the People's Bank of China.

20. In order to apply for a charter for local branches, the applicant commercial bank shall submit the following documents:

(i) A completed application form; including the name of the branch bank, total assets managed, type of business, and location of the new branch.

(ii) The most recent annual balance sheet statement of the applicant bank.

(iii) A copy of the officer's licences for top management.

(iv) A business plan.

(v) Location and security information.

(vi) Other documents as required by the People's Bank of China.

21. The approved branch will be issued an operating permit by the People's Bank of China. The branch shall then register with the local government office to receive a licence.

22. Commercial banks shall establish standard accounting and funds transfer rules among bank branches.

23. The People's Bank of China shall publish a list of the newly approved branches of commercial banks.

24. Commercial banks must obtain permission from the People's Bank of China to make the following changes:

(i) To change the bank's name;

(ii) To change registration bank capital;

(iii) To change the location of the bank headquarters or branches;

(iv) To change business types;

(v) To alter the list of shareholders who own 10 per cent or more of the bank's stock;

Appendix (*continued*)

(vi) To change any of the rules of the bank [previously approved];

(vii) To make other changes as defined by the People's Bank of China. When changing the Chairman or CEO, the new Chairman or CEO shall pass the state qualifying criteria administered by the People's Bank of China.

25. Any commercial bank split up or merger with another bank shall be done in accordance with the Company Organization Act of the People's Republic of China.

26. Commercial banks are forbidden from using fake licences, or renting or lending legitimate licences.

27. The following people shall not take a management position in commercial banks:

    (i) A person who was in prison.

    (ii) The former manager of a bankrupt company.

    (iii) The former manager of a company which has been shut down by the authorities due to the operation of an illegal business.

    (iv) A person who has a large amount of personal loans and has not paid them back.

28. Shareholders who want to buy more than 10 per cent of the commercial bank shares shall apply for approval from the People's Bank of China.

Chapter 3   Protecting the depositors

29. The commercial bank private savings deposit business shall be conducted in accordance with the desire of the depositors, allowing depositors to withdraw their deposits on demand, pay interest on savings deposits, and protect the privacy of the depositors.

30. Regarding the privacy of organization savings of industrial enterprises, the commercial bank can refuse to answer any enquiries by any other organization or person.

31. Commercial banks shall set their savings deposit interest rates in compliance with the allowed rate range established by the People's Bank of China.

32. Commercial banks shall hand in required reserves to the People's Bank of China.

33. Commercial banks must guarantee the payment of deposits plus interest upon depositors' demand.

Chapter 4   Loan business

34. Commercial banks shall develop their loan business in conformance with the states' plan for national economic and social development.

35. Commercial banks shall monitor the borrower's use of funds, repayment ability, and repayment methods. The office responsible for issuing loans shall be separated from the office that originates the loan decisions.

36. Borrowers shall provide a third party guarantee to commercial banks. Commercial banks shall check the guarantor's repayment ability, collateral value and collateral ownership. Upon assessment of the borrower's credit, the commercial bank may waive the guarantee requirement at its discretion.

37. Commercial bank loans shall be formalized in a loan contract. The loan contracts shall specify the loan type, loan usage, amount, interest rate, repayment date, and the responsibilities of both parties in the case of loan default.

38. The commercial bank's loan rate shall conform to the interest rate ranges established by People's Bank of China.

39. Commercial banks shall manage their loan business in accordance with the following balance sheet management rules:
    (i) Available cash shall not fall bellow 8 per cent of total assets.
    (ii) The ratio of total loans and total savings shall not be higher than 75 per cent.
    (iii) The ratio of short-term assets to short-term liabilities shall not be lower than 25 per cent.
    (iv) The loans to any single organization shall not be higher than 10 per cent of the bank's total assets.
    (v) Other balance sheet management rules set by the People's Bank of China.

40. Commercial banks shall not make loans directly or indirectly to persons or companies closely linked to the bank. Guarantees provided by the bank to closely linked companies shall not be superior to the guarantees provided to other non-linked companies. The term linked as applied in this act means: (a) A [business] relationship between a commercial bank manager and a relative, and (b) A relationship between a relative of a commercial bank manager and the managers of a company that the commercial bank has a lending relationship with.

41. No person or organization may require a commercial bank to make any specific loan.

42. Borrowers shall repay their loans in a timely manner. Otherwise commercial banks have the right to require the guarantor to repay the loan plus interest.

43. Commercial banks shall not engage in trust and investment activity inside the borders of the People's Republic of China, and shall not invest in real estate that is not occupied by the commercial bank itself.

44. Commercial banks shall not delay cashing cheques, transferring funds, or the collection of payments.

45. Bonds issued by commercial banks shall be approved by the authorities in advance.

46. Inter-bank borrowing shall comply with the rules of the People's Bank of China. The longest term of inter-bank borrowing allowed shall be less than four months. Commercial banks are forbidden from making loans or making investments with funds acquired through inter-bank borrowing. Funds used for inter-bank lending shall come from the funds

Appendix (*continued*)

left over after commercial banks transfer their required reserves to the Central Bank [the People's Bank of China], maintain sufficient vault cash, and repay their central bank discount loans. Funds acquired through inter-bank borrowing shall be used exclusively to make up inter-customer transaction settlement discrepancies, and to make up inter-bank payment shortfalls resulting from exchange rate movements.

47. Commercial banks shall not attract savings deposits by manipulating interest rates in violation of law.
48. Industrial enterprises may open an account in any commercial bank, but they shall not open more than one account.
49. Commercial bank business hours shall serve the convenience of customers.
50. Commercial banks may charge fees for the services they provide.
51. Commercial banks shall keep a record of all their accounting information, records of business contracts, and other documents.
52. Employees in commercial banks must obey the law and must not engage in the following behaviour:
    (i) Bribing or accepting bribes;
    (ii) Diverting bank funds or customer funds to personal accounts;
    (iii) Making loans to relatives and friends;
    (iv) Taking a management position at other enterprises;
    (v) Engaging in other illegal conduct.
53. Employees of commercial banks shall not release national or Industrial secrets.

Chapter 5   Accounting

54. Commercial banks shall set up a complete accounting system for the bank according to state laws and national standards [approved by the State Council] and other accounting rules as defined by the People's Bank of China.
55. Commercial banks shall write accounting records of the bank's business accurately and honestly, publish annual reports, and submit such accounting reports to the People's Bank of China.
56. Commercial banks shall publish financial reports for the previous fiscal year by the end of the first quarter of the next fiscal year.
57. Commercial banks shall maintain adequate amounts of cash to cover potential losses due to defaulted loans.
58. The fiscal year for commercial banks extends from 1 January to 31 December.

Chapter 6   Supervision

59. Commercial banks shall implement procedures which assure that its business is conducted according to the regulations of the People's Republic of China.

60. Commercial banks shall implement an internal audit system for savings, loans, settlement business, and for the monitoring of defaulting loans. Commercial banks shall also audit the operations of their local branches.
61. Commercial banks shall regularly submit balance sheets to the People's Bank of China, including profit-loss statements and other accounting reports.
62. The People's Bank of China shall have the right to audit the operations of commercial banks including savings, loans, clearing and 'bad'-loan business.
63. Commercials bank shall accept the supervision of the state auditing authority.

Chapter 7   Termination/takeover of commercial banking operation

64. A commercial bank may be taken over by the People's Bank of China following a credit crisis that affects the bank's ability to repay the depositors. The purpose of the takeover is to implement the steps necessary to protect depositors' legal rights, and to restart the normal operation of the bank. The debtor–creditor relationship will not be changed by the takeover.
65. The takeover of a commercial bank shall be decided by the People's Bank of China and conducted by the People's Bank of China. The official announcement of the takeover of a commercial bank shall include the following information:
    (i) The name of the commercial bank;
    (ii) The reason for the takeover;
    (iii) The organization of the process of the takeover;
    (iv) The timeframe for the takeover;
    (v) The decision shall be published openly by the People's Bank of China.
66. From the beginning of the takeover, the People's Bank of China's special takeover team shall manage the bank.
67. The People's Bank of China may grant an extension of period of time for the takeover, not to exceed two years.
68. The following conditions may cause termination of the takeover process:
    (i) The timeframe ends;
    (ii) The commercial bank recovers [from the conditions leading to the credit crisis and subsequent takeover] and can now operate normally;
    (iii) The commercial bank has been officially pronounced bankrupt.
69. When a commercial bank wants to cease its existence because it is merging with another commercial bank, or for any other reason defined by the state company laws, it must apply to the People's Bank of China for permission and submit a complete set of documents explaining how the bank will pay its depositors their principal savings plus interest. A settlement team shall than be established [within the People's Bank of China] to determine the bank's assets and liabilities. The People's Bank of China shall supervise this process of bank termination.

Appendix (*continued*)

70. When the commercial bank's licence is terminated by the People's Bank of China, the People's Bank of China shall form a settlement team to determine the bank's assets and liabilities and pay the bank's depositors their principal savings plus interest.

71. When a commercial bank is not able to pay debts, after the approval of the People's Bank of China, a local court may publicly announce that the bank is bankrupt. The court shall then organize the formation of a settlement team with the People's Bank of China to determine the bank's assets and liabilities. The bankruptcy settlement sequence shall place the highest priority on the payment of employee salaries and benefits and the costs associated with the bankruptcy, and then the repayment of savings deposits plus interest to the depositors.

72. Commercial banks may be officially terminated due to merger, termination of licence, or the announcement of bankruptcy.

Chapter 8 Legal responsibilities

73. A commercial bank that conducts its operations in an untimely manner causing a delay in payment or settlement, and such delay causes harm to its depositors, must compensate the depositors by paying interest on such deposits sufficient to cover the period of the delay of payment. A bank's payments and settlements will be considered to be untimely under the following conditions:
    (i) Delay of payment of savings deposits without for any reason;
    (ii) The refusal to cash a cheque, to accept a receipt, or delay a transaction in violation of the state's banking rules;
    (iii) The freezing, or partly freezing, of personal or organization deposits;
    (iv) Other conduct which does harm to depositors.

74. Commercial banks that engage in the following behaviour may be fined by the People's Bank of China:
    (i) Issue bank bonds or borrow funds from foreign companies without the authorization of the People's Bank of China;
    (ii) Buy and sell Chinese government bonds and foreign currency without the authorization of the People's Bank of China;
    (iii) Conduct trust and investment operations, stock investment or real estate investment within national borders;
    (iv) Invest in non-bank financial firms and industrial enterprises;
    (v) Make loans to the relatives of commercial bank officers;
    (vi) Issue fraudulent accounting reports;
    (vii) Refuse the supervision and auditing of the People's Bank of China;
    (viii) Rent or lend commercial bank licences.

75. Commercial banks that conduct untimely operations as defined in Article 73, or engage in any of the following behaviour shall be fined by the People's Bank of China:

(i) Do not pay their required reserves;

(ii) Do not comply with the balance sheet management rules defined in Article 39;

(iii) Open local branches without the permission of the People's Bank of China;

(iv) Merge with other banks without the permission of the People's Bank of China;

(v) Engage in inter-bank borrowing which exceeds the four-month limit;

(vi) Illegally increase or decrease interest rates, or engage in other illegal behaviour in order to attract savings deposits;

Source: ACFB, 1997–9. (Articles after Chapter 8 Article 75 are omitted.)

Appendix 2　Partial List of Legislation, Regulations, Policies and Major Facts Related to Chinese Financial Reforms

Year	Authorities	Legislations, regulations, policies and major facts
1948		Creation of the People's Bank of China (PBC) by merging Northern Bank, North Ocean Bank, and the Northwestern Agriculture Bank
1949		The Bank of China was spun off from PBC
1951	State	1951, 1955 and 1963 the Agriculture Bank of China came into existence three times
1952	State	The Bank of Communications was made responsible to the Ministry of Finance, and acted as the government's treasury agency for allocating capital investments
1952–5	State	All private commercial banks changed to state–private corporate banks
1954	State	Bank of Communications was superseded by PCBC
1955	State	All the state–private co-owned banks were consolidated with PBC
Dec. 1978	State	The Third Plenary Session of the 11th Communist Party Central Committee, Deng Xiao-ping proposed new legislation and plan to begin the economic reform.
1979	State	Six cities were opened for the foreign banks to set up branches.
1982	State	Twenty-three cities plus Hai Nan province were opened to the foreign banks to set up their branches.
Jan. 1983	State	Establishment of the People's Construction Bank of China (PCBC)
1984	State	Administration File Stipulating the PBC as the Central Bank of China
Jan. 1984	State	Establishment of the Chinese Industry and Commercial Bank (ICBC)
Oct. 1984	PBC	Chinese inter-bank lending market was officially approved by the PBC

Year	Authorities	Legislations, regulations, policies and major facts
1987		CITIC Industrial Bank, a famous non-state-owned commercial bank, was established. There were other city commercial banks established: Xingye Bank of Fujian Province (in November 1981), the Huitong Urban Co-operative Bank in Sichuan Province (in February 1985), the Zhao Shang Bank at Shenzhen Shekou district (in August 1986), the Development Bank of Shen Zhen City (in June 1987) and the Development Bank of Guangdong Provice (in June 1988).
1988	PBC	The Regulation of the Holdings of Cash
1990		Shanghai Stock Exchange, the first stock market in China after 1949, was established.
1992	PBC	Transforming the Management Mechanisms of State-owned Industrial Enterprises
1993	MOF	Accounting Rules for the Financial and Insurance Industries
Aug. 1993	State	The Regulation of Enterprise Debt Management
Sep. 1993	Congress*	The Anti-Trust Law of the PRC
Sep. 1993	Congress	The Law of Economic Contracts of the PRC
Sep. 1993	Congress	The Law of State Public Administrators
Mar. 1995	Congress	Act of the People's Bank of China, Legislation Passed by the People's Congress
1996	Congress	'Securities Market Act'
1996	PBC	Eight foreign banks, Bank of Tokyo/Mitsubishi, The Industry Bank of Japan, Citigroup, Hong Kong Bank, Daiichi Kangyo Bank, Shanghai-Paris International Bank, Standard Chartered Bank and Sanwa Bank were allowed to do Renminbi (RMB) business.
Jun. 1996	PBC	Announcement of PBC emphasizing monetary policy.
Jul. 1997		The Asian Financial Crisis officially began with the devaluation of the Thai baht
1998	PBC	Nine more foreign banks were allowed to collect RMB deposits and issue RMB loans in Pu Dong district of Shanghai city. Shengzhen city became the second city for the foreign banks to do RMB business.
1998	MOF	'Amendment of Regulations Governing the Calculation of Loan Maturation Time and the Withdraw of Reserve for Default Loans'
1998	MOF	'The Temporary Regulation of Setting-up Commercial Bank Fund for Default Loans'
1998	PBC	'The Regulation of Inter-bank Trading'
1998	PBC	'Regulations Governing Policy Bank Bonds'

Year	Authorities	Legislations, regulations, policies and major facts
1998	PBC	'The Regulation of Clearing Business among Banks'
May 1998	PBC	Re-established the open-market operation by trading treasury bills
Dec. 1998	Congress	Fifteen articles of the Securities Market Act were amended and passed by the Sixth Meeting of the People's Congress Standing Committee on 29 December 1998
1999	PBC	'Categorization of Loans Based on Risks'
1999	PBC	'Rules against Conduct of Cheating and Illegal Trade of Foreign Currencies'
1999	PBC	'Rules against Crimes in the Financial Markets'
1999	PBC	'The Regulation of Trading Futures'
1999	PBC	Amended the regulation of the foreign banks doing RMB business. The foreign banks are allowed to setup branches not only in the 23 cities plus Hai Nan province defined in 1996, but also in all the other major cities in China.
Aug. 1999	PBC	'Regulations Governing Brokerage Firms' Entry of Inter-bank Lending Market'
Jan. 1999	PBC	PBC restructuring, 9 new divisional branches of PBC began to work
2000	PBC	'The Regulation of Renminbi' (Chinese Currency)
Feb. 2000	PBC	'The Regulation of Brokerage Firms Obtaining Stock-backed Collateral Loans'
Jun. 2001	PBC	'Decision of Temporarily Reducing the State Holding of Stocks to Raise Funds for Social Securities'
Dec. 2001		PR China joined the WTO

*Congress: People's Congress of China.
Source: People's Bank of China, *ACFB*, various issues

Appendix 3 Administration Rules for Interest Rates (1 April 1999)

Chapter 1 General

1. The purpose of this regulation is to use interest rates to regulate economic growth. To reinforce the administration of interest rates. To protect the financial environment. To create a fair competitive environment
2. All the financial institutions, which accept deposits and grant loans in Chinese currency Renminbi will obey this regulation
3. The People's Bank of China is the administrator of the interest rates authorized by the State Council. Any group or individual should not interfere
4. The interest rates defined by the People's Bank of China are the legal interest rates. Any other group or individual cannot alter them

Chapter 2 Establishment and Administration of Interest Rates

5. The People's Bank of China sets and alters the following rates:
   1) The People's Bank of China's deposit rates, loan rates, and discount rates
   2) Deposit and loan rates of financial institutions
   3) Discount loan rates
   4) Finance charge rates
   5) Inter-bank savings rates
   6) Range of floating interest rates
   7) Other
6. Financial institutions establish the following interest rates:
   1) Floating rates
   2) Intra-bank rates
   3) Inter-bank lending rates
   4) Other rates allowed by the People's Bank of China
7. The People's Bank of China performs the following duties:
   1) Sets the interest rate regulation according to economic conditions and implements the regulation
   2) Manages branches of the People's Bank of China
   3) Monitors financial institutions obeying the interest rate regulation and policy

Appendix (*continued*)

    4) Coordinates and disciplines the financial institutions for violations
    5) Explains the interest rate policies and regulations
    6) Researches, plans and implements interest rate reform
    7) Monitors and regulates the interest rate
    8) Other

8. The branches of the People's Bank of China have the following responsibilities:
    1) Administer interest rates in the authorized areas
    2) Transfer the People's Bank of China's files and maintain confidentiality
    3) Supervise interest rates of financial institutions in authorized areas
    4) Establish systems for reporting interest rate violations
    5) Explain interest rate policies and regulations
    6) Research interest rate policies
    7) Other

9. Financial institutions have the following responsibilities:
    1) To help the People's Bank of China and administer interest rates
    2) To report to the People's Bank of China any new interest rates. If there is a discrepancy, the People's Bank of China will dictate the interest rate
    3) To do business according to interest rate regulations and laws
    4) To permit the People's Bank of China to examine interest rates
    5) To publish the interest rates in the business office
    6) To report any interest rate problems to the People's Bank of China

10. Interest rate administrators will obey rules. Should maintain confidentially and not violate rules

Chapter 3   Calculation of Interest Rates

11. The calculation of interest rates for individuals is performed according to 'Regulation of Savings'
12. The calculation of interest rates for units is performed according to 'Regulation of RMB Savings by Units'
13. The collateral collected by the People's Bank of China will be linked to savings in the unit to calculate interest rates
14. The interest rates earned by deposits are established on the day the deposits are made
15. The financial institution's reserve requirement will be calculated quarterly on the 20th of the last month of each quarter
16. The postal savings shall be calculated quarterly on the 20th of the last month of each quarter
17. The insurance companies' reserve requirement will be calculated according to the financial institutions' reserve requirement
18. The financial institutions' fiscal savings earn no interest
19. The financial institutions' inter-bank savings rates will be equal or less than the reserve requirement's rate

Chapter 4   Loan Rate Calculation

20. Short-term loan rates (less than one year) will be determined according to the rate on the signing date
21. Long-term loan rates (more than one year) will be determined annually
22. Discount rates will be calculated based on the rates on every business day
23. Trust loan rates can be negotiated by two parties under the interest rate ceiling (including float)
24. Renewal loan rates will be based on accumulated dates
25. Holders of overdue loans will pay finance charge rates starting from the first overdue date
26. Repayment of the loans before the due date may still accrue interest according to the original agreement
27. Mortgage rates are based on 'Mortgage Rates Administration Regulations'.
28. The People's Bank of China loan rates to the financial institutions are based on the agreement
29. Discount rates are based on the rate on the business day

Chapter 5   Finance Charge

30. Violations of interest rate regulations include:
    1) Increase or decrease interest rates not according to the regulations
    2) Indirectly increase or decrease interest rates not according to the regulations
    3) Issue bonds with interest rates higher than permitted
    4) Other violations
31. The People's Bank of China will discipline those who violate the above article
32. The interest received by financial firms through collecting higher than the loan rate or paying less than the deposit rate will not be protected by law. The interest received by depositors through collecting more interest than the deposit rates or pay less interest than loan rates will not be protected by law
33. If financial institutions do not pay depositors the matured deposit because of unpredicted reasons, the interest will be calculated according to the original rate
34. Enterprises which issue a bond with interest rate higher than permitted should be stopped by the branches of the People's Bank of China
35. The managers of the financial institutions which violate this regulation will be disciplined according to the 'Discipline of Violators in Financial Institutions'
36. Those receiving disciplines are permitted to report to the higher level of People's Bank of China Branch

Chapter 6   Appendix

37. This regulation is explained by the People's Bank of China
38. This regulation takes effect on April 1, 1999

Source: Interest Rates Brochure (1999).

Bibliography

ACFB   *see* People's Bank of China (1993–9, 2000–1) *ACFB*.

Allsopp, C. J. and Lin, C. (1992) 'Strengthening China's Monetary Policy and Financial Market Development', *Proceedings of International Seminar on China's Financial System Reform*. (Haikou, P.R. China).

Arestis, P. and Demetriades P. (1999) 'Financial Liberalization: The Experience of Developing Countries', *Eastern Economic Journal*, vol. 25, no. 4.

Bank of China Home Page (Internet) (1999) 'Financial System in the People's Republic of China', People's Bank of China.

Bank of Tokyo (1994) Annual Reports on the World Economy.

Bell, M. and Kochhar, K. (1992) *China – An Evolving Market Economy: A Review of Reform Experience*, IMF Working Paper WP/92/89 (December), IMF.

Blejer, M. and Szapary, G. (1989) *The Evolving Role of Fiscal Policy in Centrally Planned Economies Under Reform: The Case of China*, IMF Working Paper WP/89/26 (March), IMF.

Blejer, M. and Szapary, G. (1990) 'The Changing Role of Macroeconomic Policies in China', *Finance and Development* (June).

Bowles, Paul and White, G. (1992) 'The Dilemmas of Market Socialism: Capital Market Reform in China', *Journal of Development Studies*, vol. 28.

Bowles, Paul and White, G. (1993) *The Political Economy of China's Financial Reform in Late Development* (Oxford: Westview).

Burton, D. and Ha, Jiming (1990) *Economic Reform and the Demand for Money in China*, IMF Working Paper WP/90/42 (April), IMF.

Business Asia (1992) 'Business Outlook China', *Weekly Report to Managers of Asia/Pacific Operations*, Vol. 24, no.1, 6 January 1992.

Chan, K. Hung and Chow, Lynne (1997) 'International Transfer Pricing for Business Operations in China: Inducements, Regulation and Practice', *Journal of Business Finance and Accounting*, vol. 24, no. 9.

Chen, Songlin (2001) 'The Impact of Monetary Policy when a Loan Enters the Stock Market', *Chinese Finance*, vol.4.

Chen, Xiaowei (1994) 'A Summary of Discussion on China's Inflation Among the Chinese Economists in Recent Years', *Finance and Trade Economics*, vol.11.

China Statistics Yearbook (Zhongguo Tongji Nianjian) various issues from 1990 to 2001 (Beijing: China Financial Publishing House).

China-window.com News Co. (1998) 'Chinese Central Banking Reform is Making Progress: Nine Branches of the Central Bank are Established' (Internet) 31 December, 1998.

Chinese LA Daily News (1998) 'The Discussion over the Devaluation of the Chinese Currency Renminbi', (Internet) 16 November 1998. El Monte, CA. Tel: (818) 453–8800.

Dai, Xianglong (2002) Press Conference of Chairman of PBC, 15 January, Chinese Central Television 4.

Davies, Keri (1994) 'Foreign Investment in the Retail Sector of The People's Republic of China', *Columbia Journal of World Business* (Fall).

De Wulf, Luc and Goldsbrough, D. (1986) 'Evolving Role of Monetary Policy in China' IMF Working Paper, vol.33, no.2 (June) Washington DC, IMF.

Deng, Shimin (2001) 'Shareholding Commercial Banking Reform and Development', *Chinese Finance*, vol. 4.

Dickie, P. (1997) 'Toward Resilient Financial Systems', in *Creating Resilient Financial Regimes in Asia: Challenges and Policy Options* (Oxford University Press).

Dornbusch, R. (1998) *Macroeconomics*, 7th edn (New York: McGraw-Hill Co).

Economic Research Institute of Beijing University, '1998 Monetary Policy Review and the Forecast of 1999', *Journal of Finance* published by the Chinese Finance Association, 18 December 1998.

Fan, G. and Schaffer, M. (1992) 'Decentralized Socialism and Macroeconomic Stability: Lessons from China', Dept. of Economics, Univ. of California at Davis, Working Paper Series no. 411.

Financial Times (6 January 2000) 'Chinese Central Bank Shifts Trading Stance' by James Kynge in Beijing.

Folkerts-Landau, David (1993) *Payment System Reform in Formerly Centrally Planned Economies* (Washington, DC: International Monetary Fund).

Gao, C. (2001) 'How to Assess the Impact of Bad Loans on Inflation and Monetary Policies', *Chinese Finance*, vol. 5.

Gautier, J. (1990) 'Financial Reform, Financial Policy, and Bank Regulation', *The Evolving Role of Central Banks* (IMF).

Girardin, Eric (1997) 'The Structure and Dynamics of Financial Institutions in China' in *Banking Sector Reform and Credit Control in China* (Paris, France: OECD Development Center).

Hicks, John (1937) 'Mr. Keynes and the Classics: A Suggested Interpretation', *Econometrica*: 147–59.

Horiguchi, Y. and Deppler, M. (1993) 'Case Studies of China and Poland', in R. C. Borth *et al. Proceedings of Seminar: Coordinating Stabilization and Structural Reform* (Washington, DC: IMF).

Interest Rates Brochure (1999) People's Bank of China, Wuhan Branch.

International Conference on Monetary Policy (2001) 'Monetary Policy Operation', *Chinese Finance*, vol. 6.

International Financial Statistics (2000) (World Bank). March issue.

Jefferson, G. H. and Rawski, T. G. (1994) 'Enterprise Reform in Chinese Industry', *Journal of Economic Perspectives*, vol.8, no.2 (Spring).

Jin, L. (1994) *Monetary Policy and the Design of Financial Institutions in China 1978–1990* (London and New York: St Antony's/Macmillan).

Johnston, R. (1990) 'Sequencing Financial Reform' in *The Evolving Role of Central Banks* (Washington, DC: IMF).

Katz, S. S. (1999) 'The Asian Crisis, the IMF and the Critics', *Eastern Economic Journal*, vol. 25, no. 4.

Khor, H. E. (1991) *China: Macroeconomic Cycles in the 1980s*, IMF Working Paper WP/91/85 (September).

Lardy, Nicholas R. (1993) 'China as a NIC', *International Economic Insights*, vol. 4, no.3 (May/June).

Lardy, Nicholas R. (1995) *The World of Banking* (Lake Forest, IL: Financial Publishing Co.).

Lee, John W. S. (2000) 'Banking Reform in China (1978–1998)', *Asian Profile*, vol. 28, no. 3.

Li, Maosheng (1987) *Studies on China's Financial Structure* (Xi'an and Beijing: Shannxi People's Press).

Li, Shourong (1993) *General Studies on China's Financial System* (Beijing: Chinese Economics Management Press).

Li, Xiao-xi (1991) *Comparison Study of Modern Inflation Theories* (Beijing: Chinese Social Science Press).

Li, Zhonglin, Qiao, Xudong, and Hangxiang Jiang (2001) 'The Improvement in China's Preparation Fund for Default Loans, using International Examples', *Chinese Finance*, vol. 4.

Lin, Zhimin (1994) 'Reform and Shanghai: Changing Central–Local Fiscal Relations' in Jia Hao (ed.) *Changing Central–Local Relations in China: Reform and State Capacity* (Boulder, CO: Westview).

Liu, Guangdi (1984) *Banks in China* (Beijing: Beijing Press).

Liu, Qiusheng (1993) 'On the Effect of Monetary Policy in Recent Years', *Finance Studies*, no. 4.

Lou, Jiwei and Gao, Jianhong (1994) 'Reform of Monetary Policy Instruments of the Central Bank and the Development of the State Debt Market', *Finance and Trade Economics*, vol. 1.

Lu, M. and Timmer, P. (1992) 'Developing the Chinese Rural Economy: Experience of the 1980s and Prospects for the Future', HIID Development Discussion Paper no. 428.

Luo, Lan (2001) 'Principles and Implementation of Market Oriented Interest Rates', *Chinese Finance*, vol. 3.

Ma, Hong and Sun, Shangqing (1991) *China's Economic Situation and Prospects, 1990–1991* (Beijing: China Development Press).

McGill, Peter (1993) 'Shanghai Bids to Become a Top Financial Center', *Euromoney* (April).

McKinnon, R. I. (1973) *Money and Capital in Economic Development* (Washington, DC: Brookings Institution).

McKinnon, R. I. (1993) *The Order of Economic Liberalization: Financial Control in the Transition to a Market Economy* (Baltimore and London: Johns Hopkins University Press).

Mishkin, Frederic S. (1998) *The Economics of Money, Banking and Financial Markets*, 5th edn (Addison-Wesley).

Naughton, B. (1994) 'Implications of the State Monopoly Over Industry and its Relaxation', *Modern China* vol. 18, no.1.

Nuti, D. M. (1989) 'Remonetization and the Capital Market in the Reform of Centrally Planned Economics', *European Economic Review*, vol. 33.

Peebles, G. (1991) *Money in the People's Republic of China: A Comparative Perspective* (North Sydney, NSW: Allen and Unwin).

People's Bank of China (1993–1999, 2000–1) *ACFB: Almanac of China's Finance and Banking*, various issues.

People's Bank of China (1993–1999) *China Monthly Statistics Summary* (various issues).

People's Bank of China (1993a) 'Ten Regulations Preventing the Hiking of Interest Rates' (June).

People's Bank of China (1993b) 'Some Opinions Regarding the Current Economic Situation', Document No. 15.

People's Bank of China (1995a) 'Act of the People's Bank of China', Legislation Passed by the People's Congress, 18 March 1995 (published 10 May 1995).

People's Bank of China (1995b) 'The Commercial Banks Act of The People's Republic of China', Legislation Passed by People's Congress, 10 May 1995.

People's Bank of China (2002) official website http://www.stats.gov.cn/ndsj/zgnj/2000/C01c.htm–data as of may 2002.

People's Daily (1987) 'Report of the First Plenary Session of the 13th Communist Party Central Committee', October.

People's Daily (1992) 'Report of Jiang Ze-min, President of China, in the First Plenary Session of the 14th Communist Party Central Committee, October.

Perkins, Dwight (1994) 'Completing China's Move to the Market', Journal of Economic Perspectives, vol. 8, no. 2.

Poole, William (1970) 'Optimal Choice of Monetary Policy Instruments in a Simple Stochastic Macro Model', Quarterly Journal of Economics, May–June.

Qian, Ying-Yi (1988) 'Urban and Rural Household Savings in China', IMF Staff Papers vol. 35, no. 4.

Rawski, Thomas G. (1991) 'How Fast Has Chinese Industry Grown?' Research Paper Series, no. 7, Socialist Economies Reform Unit, Country Economics Department, World Bank.

Rawski, Thomas G. (1993) 'An Overview of Chinese Industry in the 1980s', University of Pittsburg Seminar.

Rondinelli, Dennies A. (1993) 'Resolving US–China Trade Conflicts', Columbia Journal of World Economy, Summer.

Root, H. L. (1994) 'Information Asymmetry in Chinese Financial Markets: Political Risk and Financial Intermediation in PR China' in Proceedings of International Conference on Financing the Development of Guangdong, 12–14 December.

Sachs, J. (1988) 'Conditionality, Debt Relief and the Developing Countries' Debt Crisis', in J. Sachs (ed.) Developing Country Debt and Economic Performance (Chicago: University of Chicago Press).

Santorum, A. (1993) 'China 1949–1988', in S. Page (ed.) Monetary Policy in Developing Countries (London: Routledge).

Shanghai-Window.com News Co. (1998) 'The First Case of Allowing Foreign Banks to Deal with Chinese Currency Business', 22 December.

Shaw, E. S. (1973) Financial Deepening in Economic Development (New York: Oxford University Press).

State Council document (1991) Chinese State Council document 71.

State Council document (1997) Chinese State Council document 15.

Taiwan Today News Network (1998) 'The People's Republic of China Passed the Legislation on Security Market in order to fight with the International Hedge Fund' (Internet) 24 December.

Tam, On-Kit (1988) 'Issues in Developing of China's Financial Reform', Finance and Economics (Cai Jin Ke Xue), no.2.

Theil, H. (1964) Optimal Decision Rules for Government and Industry (Amsterdam: North-Holland).

Tobin, J. (1984) 'On the Efficiency of the Financial System', Lloyds Bank Review, no. 153 (July).

Tsang, S. (1990) 'Controlling Money During Socialist Economic Reform: The Chinese Experience', *Economy and Society*, vol. 19, no. 2.

Wang, Hauqing (2001) 'The Monetary Policy Operation Mode during the Reform', *Chinese Finance*. Vol.7.

Wang, Zhouxin(1993) 'The Transition From Direct Financial Control to Indirect Adjustment', *Finance and Trade Economics*, no.8.

World Bank (1988) *World Development Report* (Oxford: Oxford University Press).

World Bank (1989) *World Development Report* (Oxford: Oxford University Press).

World Bank (1993) *The East Asian Miracle: Economic Growth and Public Policy* (Oxford: Oxford University Press).

World Bank (1994) *China: Country Economic Review* (Oxford: Oxford University Press).

World Bank (1997) *International Banking and Financial Crisis* (Oxford: Oxford University Press).

Wu, Jinglian (1995) 'Industrial Financing and Credit Expansion', *Chinese Finance*, vol.4.

Xie, Duo (2001) 'China Currency Market Development' *Chinese Finance* vol. 7.

Xie, H. (1999) 'Financial Corporations in China: Characteristics, Problems and Policy Implementation', *Finance Study Journal*, vol. 3 (in Chinese).

Xu, Xiaoping (1998) 'Chapter 1: Monetary Policy and Macroeconomic Stability', 'Chapter 2: Monetary Policy Instruments and Their Limits', *China's Financial System under Transition*. (New York: St Martin's Press).

Yang, Haiqun (1996) *Banking and Financial Control in Reforming Planned Economies* (London: Macmillan).

Yusuf, Shahid (1994) 'China's Macroeconomic Performance and Management During Transition', *Journal of Economic Perspectives*, vol. 8, no. 2.

Zheng, C. (1999) 'The Theory Frame of Chinese Inflation Analysis', *Finance Study Journal*, vol. 3 (in Chinese).

Zhang, H. (2001) 'Analysis of the Money Supply in 2000', *Chinese Finance*, vol.4.

Zhang, Yi-Chen and Da Yu (1994) 'China's Emerging Securities Market', *Columbia Journal of World Business*, Summer.

Zhang, Wenhong (2001) 'Financial Market Analysis – the First Three Quarters 2001', *Chinese Finance*, vol. 11.

Zhou, Daojiong (1997) 'The Developing Securities Market in China', *The World of Banking* (Lake Forest, IL: Financial Publishing Co.) May–June.

Index